What People Are Saying ...

"Priya has written an insightful and compassionate book for the individual who struggles with wanting to make everyone else happy, but who neglects their own self-worth and joy. The author shares, with vulnerability, her own journey to giving herself permission to live HER life and provides useful information and tools on how to break free of the shackles which hold you back. Through thoughtful guidance, concepts, and exercises she becomes your personal guide as you take back your life." **– Shawn Achor, NY Times bestselling author of *Before Happiness* and *The Happiness Advantage***

"During my elite Olympic career which spanned over 20 years I met many people and I can say without a shadow of a doubt that Priya is one of the most genuine people I have ever met. As a client of Priya's, I was thrilled when I heard that she had decided to publish her philosophy as a comprehensive, step-by-step book ... I have no doubt that people from all walks of life will benefit from the gems in this book. Take the Permission Journey with Priya and discover that personal happiness is acceptable and completely attainable." **– Tasha Danvers, Two-time Olympian, Olympic medalist and author**

"Priya has an evident passion for her work and has put together a self-help programme with a great deal of thought and experience" **– Alexandra Shulman, editor-in-chief, British Vogue and author**

Not since Eckhart Tolle's *A New Earth* has there been such a clear description and walk-through of a healthy sense of self. Priya's work is easily understood, yet forcefully intelligent. Her well-integrated use of personal testimony makes this one of the most thoughtful and revealing books in the self-help genre. A must-read for those at any sort of crossroads in life." **– Dr. Steven Berry, pastor, author and founder of Global Meetinghouse Enterprises**

"Give YourSelf Permission to Live Your Life will get you to a place where you will genuinely believe in yourself enough to take the calculated risks needed to be successful in any adventure you chose to participate in … The Permission Journey™ will help you master a stable work/life balance so you can get on with it and achieve the triumphs you deserve! I am blessed to count Priya as a close friend and I cannot recommend anyone more highly – you will love this book!" **– Deri Ap-John Llewelyn Davies AKA The Strategy Man, International speaker and best selling author**

"Give YourSelf Permission to Live Your Life truly reached out to me in such a deep and personal way. Priya Rana Kapoor will take readers by the hand and masterfully lead them on a journey that will not only strengthen their mindset, improve their relationships, reinforce their dreams, but most importantly - give them permission to be happy. This book is now a cornerstone of my personal library." **– Matt Patterson, Inspirational Speaker and Award-Winning/Best-Selling author of** *My Emily*

"…While reading, I found myself in a mental dialogue with the text - as if having a conversation with Priya. The honesty of the text helped me … form a personal connection with the advice on each page, truly penetrating my understanding of it's meaning and how it pertains to my life…" **– Darya Zakharova, Private Banker**

Give YourSelf
Permission
to Live Your Life

Priya Rana Kapoor

BALBOA.
PRESS

A DIVISION OF HAY HOUSE

Balboa Press books may be ordered through booksellers or by contacting:

Balboa Press
A Division of Hay House
1663 Liberty Drive
Bloomington, IN 47403
www.balboapress.com
1 (877) 407-4847

Because of the dynamic nature of the Internet, any web addresses or links contained in this book may have changed since publication and may no longer be valid. The views expressed in this work are solely those of the author and do not necessarily reflect the views of the publisher, and the publisher hereby disclaims any responsibility for them.

The author of this book does not dispense medical advice or prescribe the use of any technique as a form of treatment for physical, emotional, or medical problems without the advice of a physician, either directly or indirectly. The intent of the author is only to offer information of a general nature to help you in your quest for emotional and spiritual well-being. In the event you use any of the information in this book for yourself, which is your constitutional right, the author and the publisher assume no responsibility for your actions.

Any people depicted in stock imagery provided by Thinkstock are models, and such images are being used for illustrative purposes only. Certain stock imagery © Thinkstock.

Printed in the United States of America.

ISBN: 978-1-4525-9368-5 (sc)
ISBN: 978-1-4525-9369-2 (hc)
ISBN: 978-1-4525-9367-8 (e)

Library of Congress Control Number: 2014903960

Balboa Press rev. date: 07/18/2014

for my grandmother, Ruth C. Cole

Nana, I love and miss you

Contents

Introduction xi

Prologue xvii

Chapter One

Why We Don't Give OurSelves Permission 1

What Does "Give YourSelf Permission" Mean? 3

What Is Stopping Us? 5

The Role of Personal Responsibility 11

Baby Steps 13

Where Do We Go from Here? 14

Chapter Two

The Legacy of Childhood – My Story, Part One 15

Family Tree 16

Smoke and Mirrors 18

Sleeping on Couches 20

Goodbye 22

Time for Change 24

Charmed Life 24

The Tipping Point 26

Chapter Three

The Permission Journey 29

Trains, Planes, and Automobiles 30

Chapter Four

Giving Myself Permission – My Story, Part Two 37

Taking Back My Life 37

Stumbling upon My Purpose 38

Moving Away 41

On the Ledge 42

Taking Personal Responsibility 43

Spreading My Wings.. 45

Everything Happens for a Reason 46

Where I Landed 46

Chapter Five

Give YourSelf Permission to Know You Matter

Give YourSelf Permission to Know You Matter 49

The Evolution of Knowing You Matter........................ 51

Feeling like a Fraud.. 58

Defensiveness Rearing Its Ugly Head 58

Our Bodies as a Barometer for Our Lives 60

Celebrate Your Achievements 61

Know You Matter 62

Chapter Six

Give YourSelf Permission to Know What You Care About 65

Core Values.. 67

Values as a Road Map 70

Values in Relationships 71

Why We Need to Value Ourselves 74

Other Ways to Explore Your Values 75

Know Your Values 76

Chapter Seven

Give YourSelf Permission to Take Back Your Life 79

Your Best PR.. 79

Control.. 82

How to Identify What You Can Control 84

The Blame Game... 87

Moving Away from Guilt 89

Sweeping Your Side of the Street............................... 94

Take Back Your Life 96

Chapter Eight

Give YourSelf Permission to Be Brave...................................99

    Acknowledging Your Feelings 100

    Learn to Trust... 101

    A Reality Check.. 106

    Letting Go and Forgiveness...111

    The Beauty of Resilience..114

    Risk-taking...116

    Don't Be Afraid of Success...119

    Be Brave... 120

Chapter Nine

Give YourSelf Permission to be Happy............................... 123

    It's Your Choice 123

    Tolerance versus Acceptance..126

    The Art of Positive Thinking... 128

    It's All About Mindset 137

    Give YourSelf Permission to Have Fun 139

    Don't Worry, Be Happy 141

Chapter Ten

Give YourSelf Permission to Have Healthy Relationships 143

    What Is a Healthy Relationship?..143

    What Needs to Come First? 145

    Don't Compare Your Insides with Everyone Else's Outsides............... 146

    Communicating with Others...147

    Respecting Others' Agendas 150

    Childhood Baggage 154

    Trusting Others to Make Their Own Choices...........................157

    How Our Behaviour Affects Others 159

    The Choices We Make...161

    Be in Healthy Relationships 162

Chapter Eleven

Give YourSelf Permission to Know Your Dream Team 165

    Your Foundational Dream Team 166

    Your Current Dream Team 171

    Your Inspirational Dream Team...174

    Streamlining Your Dream Team...176

    You as a Dream Team Member 177

    When Strength Is a Weakness...179

    Know Your Dream Teams 180

Chapter Twelve

Give YourSelf Permission to Dream Big and Live Your Life............ 183

    Definition of a Dream.. 183

    Why Is Dreaming Big So Difficult? 184

    The Foundations of Dreaming Big...................................... 186

    Whose Dream Is It Anyway?.. 189

    The Pitfalls... 192

    Dreamy Umbrellas 193

    Moving from Dreaming to Doing.. 194

    A Shortcut: The Permission Trifecta.................................. 196

    Staying True to Yourself 199

    Holding On to Your Intention 200

    Jedi Mind Tricks.. 201

    When Things Change 203

    Give YourSelf Permission to Live Your Life 204

Conclusion..207

    Freedom Is Yours.. 207

Epilogue... 211

Further Reading.. 213

Acknowledgements... 217

About the Author 219

Introduction

M any people are in careers and lives they feel they never completely chose for themselves. Suddenly, they see that many of the decisions they've made over the years were done in an effort to fit in or gain approval. Some made choices based upon what they believed their parents or society had told them were appropriate or worthy. Somewhere along the line, they stopped following their own hearts. One decision led to another, and they lost track of the hopes and dreams they had in early adulthood. They thought that by putting themselves first they were acting selfishly. They hoped that by conforming they were making the right decisions – maybe the easier ones. However, somewhere deep down, they now battle with the insidious feeling that they are not as happy or fulfilled as they could be. They are in a place where they no longer even allow themselves to think about what they might want to do or be.

I have been lucky enough to work with a wide range of amazing clients: people from different ethnic backgrounds, professions, and life experiences; men and women, young and old. The issues they've worked through are similarly diverse. They all have their own stories, wants, needs, and fears, and they bring those with them as they travel this life journey. Not one is the same as any other, yet over the years, I've noticed that many share one very interesting characteristic: they're not giving themselves permission to live their best lives. This controversial but simple concept lies at the root of all sorts of other issues that often cause difficulty and stress. This challenging phrase can stand between them and the lives they feel they just might deserve.

In seminars, workshops, and in individual coaching sessions, I regularly address the concept of personal responsibility. I strongly believe that we are all leaders of our own lives, and that we have the power and responsibility to take action to make change. Of course, we have responsibilities to others and to society as a whole, but we have the ultimate say in what happens in our lives. Things out of our control may happen to us, but we can decide how we react to or feel about them and how we move forward. This is not immediately evident to many, and sometimes we give away this personal power.

Ever since I can remember, I have wanted to write a book. It seemed like a calling. I had quite a colourful upbringing, and I often thought that it would make a good story. Of course, I imagined I would write it as fiction, as no one would believe all my family's adventures, and there was no way I was going to air out our dirty laundry.

But after my MS diagnosis and an encounter with a man named Joe Allen, I saw everything in a different light, and things started to change for me. I formally trained as a psychotherapist and then decided to do a life-coaching course, as I liked the forward focus and goal-setting aspect of coaching. It soon became clear that my life's purpose and work would centre on guiding people to empower themselves and encouraging people to seek their own freedom.

I finally came to understand that by sharing my story and those of some of my clients, alongside a few concepts, tools, and exercises in a personal development book, I might be able to help others.

I knew I wanted to write a book to support people facing the same kinds of hurdles as my clients, but it wasn't until I had dinner with two of my oldest friends and one of their business associates that I got the fundamental concept for this book. I mentioned that I was writing on empowerment but that I was struggling to identify the salient component. Jim, my friends' colleague, asked me what the one thing was that got in the way of people empowering themselves. Without skipping a beat, I said, "They don't give themselves permission." Then my friend Crispin said, "There you have it; that should be in the title." At that point, it all became clear. It was then that *"Give YourSelf* Permission to Live Your Life"* was born.

If we listen carefully to those in business, politics, and the self-help and personal development arenas, we hear them tell people to give themselves permission, but I would argue that some of their audience might just not know how to. And that is why I have written this book, which is all about the quiet side of empowerment, or coming into empowerment through the back door.

---

* Note on why I have capitalised the 'S' in *Give YourSelf Permission*. Honestly as I was outlining the book, it just came to me. I shortened each chapter and concept to GYSP to... and it stuck. I like the treatment and I feel that it differentiates the concept from the norm. Also, the 'Self' is a large part of the journey and what I write about, so I wanted to highlight it. Many have said it is jarring; this is why I am only using it in titles, headers, as part of *the Permission Journey* and in other obvious places, but not part of the basic text.

There comes a point when people reach a place where they realise it is time to challenge the status quo. They know that in their heart of hearts that something needs to change, but they have no idea where to start.

Since you have picked up this book, you probably already know that something is not working in your life and that you both want and need to fix it. It may have taken you a while to reach this realisation. Perhaps now you are finally ready to talk about it or to start making changes, even if you don't yet know how. Showing up is a big step and arguably the most important one.

My clients often need to learn how to listen to themselves, value themselves, and do little things to prove to themselves that their opinions and needs matter, before they embark on fulfilling their individual goals and dreams. *"Give YourSelf Permission to Live Your Life"* incorporates a step-by-step process called the Permission Journey™ which systematically will guide you through what many of my clients have already experienced. These techniques and concepts have allowed them to flourish and lead much happier lives. Lives where they are also in much healthier relationships.

I do not want to tell you what to do, but I do want to share my experience, education, and knowledge with you. My hope is that some part of what I have picked up along the path as a therapist, life coach, constant student, and inquisitive human being will resonate with you in some small way and that you will learn some skills that will enrich your life.

My vision for you is that you arrive at some awareness for yourself in the hope that you will see things a little differently. Ideally by the end of this book you will think and feel that you have every right to your dreams, goals, and aspirations. You will have given yourself permission to try a few of the techniques described and feel more empowered. In time, the goal would be that you'll unconsciously start integrating a more supportive and positive mindset into your everyday life until you are wholeheartedly living without guilt, with minimal conflict, and in harmonious relationships with your family, friends, co-workers, and all of the amazing characters you have the privilege of meeting in your lifetime.

Prologue

My husband and I arrived in Cairo the day sixty-two tourists were massacred in Luxor. We were on our honeymoon. Most countries sent a few 747s to evacuate their nationals – for some reason, the United States did not. When I called the embassy the next day, I was told not to consider travelling into Upper Egypt. That was all they recommended, and I really wasn't going to have any of that. I had wanted to explore the Valley of the Kings my whole life, so we were going to forge ahead no matter who or what got in our way!

The next morning, I woke up with numbness in my left hand. I thought I had just slept on it funny, but it continued to get worse. After ten days in Egypt, I was numb down my whole left side, was having trouble holding my head up, and was finding it difficult to walk. We cut our honeymoon short. As soon as we landed in Los Angeles, we went straight to the acute care department of the local university hospital. After being admitted for a few tests, I was told I had a demyelinating disease – whatever that was. A few years later, I was diagnosed with multiple sclerosis.

By the time we returned home from Cairo, I was having trouble moving properly. I couldn't feed myself or feel my feet on the ground or my head on the pillow. The steroids I had been prescribed resulted in horrendous nightmares and side effects. It was often easier to stay up all night watching documentaries on the atrocities at Auschwitz than to try to sleep. The medicine made me very agitated, and my cheeks blew up like those of a little chipmunk. I grew a moustache, and the lining of my mouth sloughed off. On the bright side, the obsessive-compulsive traits associated with these steroids allowed me to get all my wedding thank-you notes done and my Christmas shopping finished with plenty of time to spare. I was a newlywed, and this was supposed to be the happiest time in my life, but instead I felt terrible, and I was scared and confused.

Illness is an odd thing, especially when the disease strikes a relatively young person. I was twenty-seven. Many are faced with their own mortality earlier than they would like. Some of my friends had trouble knowing how to be there for me, and others just couldn't be. It's all very awkward.

This was my first major flare-up, and after coming home from the hospital, I had to take time off work. I was working in the admissions office of one of the largest, most elite universities in California: the University of Southern California (USC). It was December, and the first large wave of student applications had just come in.

People at work had been worried when they found out we had arrived in Egypt the day of the massacre and were even more concerned when they heard I was sick. We had very few answers at the time, so people really didn't know what to do. But then I got a call from the grand pooh-bah at work, a wonderful man by the name of Joe Allen. He was a vice provost of the university, and hundreds of employees answered to him. I had always liked and respected him greatly.

Joe insisted on coming to see me. His persistence amazed me, as I felt that I was such a small cog in the workings of the university. We sat and chatted for four hours! He didn't try to force me to be cheerful or talk me into making choices then and there. He simply gave me the space I needed to talk about what was happening to me as much or as little as I wanted to do. I remember wondering why he was staying so long and worrying that I was keeping him from his important work. It was a Friday afternoon, and I knew that everyone at the university had had a very tough week. Maybe he needed this quiet and thought-collecting time as much as I needed his care and presence.

By the time my visitor left, I was utterly exhausted, but something inside of me had changed. There was a settled peace within me. I reflected on our conversation and the time we had spent together, and I can still clearly remember thinking, "I must be *worth* something if he came to visit and stayed with me that long."

That afternoon changed my life. Joe had given me an amazing gift – the permission to think I might just be worth something – and I needed that more than anything in the world. It felt good, it felt kind, and it felt empowering. I became aware of a new resolve not to let my currently difficult situation take over, not to live as a victim, to live the way I wanted and not how others wanted me to. Not only that, but he had given me permission to start looking at what I wanted in life. I hold on to that to this day. Really, all Joe had done was visit me over a cup of tea —yet this had made all the difference.

Three years later, Joe had a stroke and died at the age of fifty-three. Anytime I tell this story, think of him, or think about where my whole journey began, I am brought to tears.

CHAPTER ONE

Why We Don't Give OurSelves Permission

Awareness is fifty percent of growth.
—Louise L. Hay

Jack: A Story of Not Giving Oneself Permission

Meet Jack.[1] He is thirty-six years old, and his life revolves around working relentlessly for the pay cheque he brings home every month. There are days when he looks in the mirror and doesn't even recognise himself in the life he has created.

Let's see how Jack got to where he is today.

Shortly after graduating from university, Jack found himself working for a good company and on track for a great career.

---

[1]   All client names and select scenarios have been changed to preserve people's privacy and mask their true identity.

He liked his job and worked hard during the week but took time for himself as well. A couple of nights a week, he went out with his friends, played sports, and sometimes had a drink or two. Jack felt really good about his choices, and he was happy to know how proud his parents were of his achievements.

Jack was doing so well at work that he was promoted. He was given more responsibilities and took on more managerial duties. He met a woman, fell in love, and got married. He was earning a great salary and was able to buy a house and a car.

Jack and his wife wanted to give their children the best of everything and thus sent them to good schools. His wife gave up her job to stay at home and take care of them. The other kids at school came from wealthy families. They went on fancy holidays, and Jack's children wanted to do the same. Whilst Jack's work was still going well, he felt under enormous pressure to keep the money rolling in.

One day, Jack realised that he was just not happy.

Now, he is still a good manager, and he still earns a good salary, so why does Jack feel so miserable most of the time? He feels as though he is being pulled in all directions and has lost control of his life. Does he even enjoy his work anymore? He doesn't think so, but he's not sure. The stress of keeping up is starting to wear him down, and he has begun to fight with his wife. She always seems to want him to be more … something, but she is struggling with her own issues too. Jack is just trying to stay above water. He has no idea what he really likes doing. He misses working with his hands; he used to create things and tinker with electronics with his dad in the shed on weekend afternoons. But Jack feels he has absolutely no time for himself anymore. When he is at home, the family wants to socialise with their neighbours, but he resists because he's so tired after a long day in the office. He feels bad about it, and he can see that his family is upset with him and disappointed because he doesn't seem to understand their needs. He is utterly fed up.

With so many things apparently going well, why is Jack so unhappy?

Rather than giving himself permission to really think about what he wants for his life, Jack's experience has been like riding a train rather than driving a car. He got on but he doesn't feel that he's dictating the direction it's going. The train whizzes by all sorts of interesting places, but it never stops for him to get off and take a look around. Jack feels as though he will never get off. He wonders at what point he lost control of his life and how he can get back in the driver's seat.

If you've ever felt as though you've been on a train that seems to be heading towards a destination you didn't choose, you are, unfortunately, not alone.

What Does "Give YourSelf Permission" Mean?

The word *permission* is used a lot in the self-help and personal development industry, in product- and service-driven businesses, in politics – really, all over the place – but what does it mean?

I use the concept of giving yourself permission to describe what happens when you decide and allow yourself to do what is best for you, whether that is saying *no* to a needy friend, taking care of your immediate needs so you can be more present with your relationships, or sometimes even *allowing* yourself to think about what you might want to do with your life. This all sounds simple enough, but consistently people balk at the very idea. At points I have suggested to some clients that they are not giving themselves permission to be their best. Their initial response is often to reject the notion completely.

"Why would I do that?" they say. "That doesn't make any sense! Who would not let themselves follow their dreams?"

They are correct; it doesn't make sense. And still, this is exactly what we do. We think we want something, but for some reason, we hold ourselves back from taking the steps necessary to achieve it.

A huge number of personal development books and programs are successful at giving you tools to empower yourself on the outside. They often encourage people to attempt quite daring feats such as bungee jumping or climbing some very high mountain. All of this is part of a process of goal setting and action planning, and the idea is for people to make very ambitious goals and then work hard to realise them.

It is all valid work, but I would argue that for many people, something else has to happen first. Long before they reach the stage of even being *able* to vocalise their long-term goals, many people need to build firm foundations of confidence and self-worth that will enable them to take the reins of personal responsibility and give themselves permission to *start* looking at what they want for their lives. They need to learn how to give themselves permission to make small advances before they're able to make great strides. Those tentative steps forward are often the hardest steps of all to take but are the ones that illicit the most satisfaction when achieved and which lead to greater long-term sustainability of new habits and behaviour. And, far from being selfish, people also become better friends, partners, sons, daughters, siblings, and co-workers.

In modern society, we usually think of permission in terms of someone else granting us the authority to do something. A passport allows us to get on a plane and enter another country, and a driving license lets us take to the roads. However, it is now time for you to give *yourself* that passport which will grant *you* the permission to travel to places unknown, the license to take care of yourself, and the liberty to be creative and free.

At this point, let's pull everything apart, then very quickly we will build it all back up again – but this time in a more fulfilling way for you. Without a little understanding as to how and why we got ourselves into this predicament, it will be more difficult to lay that very solid foundation that will allow us to build the house that will stand for many years and multiple generations. How we live our lives today dictates the legacy we pass on.

What Is Stopping Us?

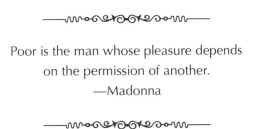

Poor is the man whose pleasure depends
on the permission of another.
—Madonna

So why *aren't* we letting ourselves do and be who we want to be? It seems counter-intuitive, doesn't it? There are many reasons we don't give ourselves permission to do certain things, and here are a few of the main ones. Have no fear, once we look at why we are holding ourselves back we will look at each issue again in the subsequent chapters and explore ways to rid ourselves of these blocks.

Fear

The main reason people don't give themselves permission to live authentically or to make decisions that are in their best interest is because they're afraid. They fear what others will think, fear taking risks that may lead to failure or making a mistake, fear the unknown, or fear being selfish. These fears hold them back from taking the biggest risk of all – living their own lives. Essentially, we feel fear because we don't believe in our abilities and ourselves.

Others

When we were children and we were given a gold star at school, we couldn't wait to get home and show it to Mum and Dad, and as adults, we still want the people in our lives to be pleased with who we are and what we do.

Many go through life worrying about what other people think of them, whether they're doing the right thing, or whether they're living up to others' expectations of them. They choose what they will and will not do based on what they perceive others will approve of.

When we're being honest, most of us will admit that we care very deeply about what others think of us. Humans are social animals, after all – being connected to others is fundamental to our species.[2]

Many prioritise others' opinions of their achievements – or what they imagine those opinions to be – over their own. They choose careers, relationships, or lifestyles not on the basis of what they want and need but what they think others want and need from them. Other times, rather than explicitly trying to please their families or other important people in their lives, people focus on trying to impress society as a whole. When they worry about what others think, they perceive that they are under constant judgement, and this makes them feel quite

---

[2]   "Matrix of Needs and Satisfiers" in M. Max-Neef, *Human Scale Development: Conception, Application and Further Reflections*, The Apex Press (1991), http://www.alastairmcintosh.com/general/resources/2007-Manfred-Max-Neef-Fundamental-Human-Needs.pdf.

vulnerable, which is an emotion or trait many would rather not feel and would sooner hide.

In their quest to be accepted, they often lose sight of what they really want in life. They can get to a point where they're even afraid to think or dream of what they want for themselves, and at the same time, they relinquish the responsibility for achieving it. They spend so long trying to live up to what they suppose others' expectations for them are that they forget their own dreams completely and don't make a change for fear of disappointing someone.

They often put themselves last because they don't value or truly care about themselves. They look for safety from those around them and don't allow themselves to achieve all that they truly believe they can. By seeking permission, approval, and positive feedback from others, they place themselves in a subordinate position.

Change

Many people experience a profound and disabling fear of change. On the surface, they're afraid of change itself and worry about what might happen or what people will think of them if they evolve and become different.

I've worked with many clients who carry a lot of guilt because their parents have always wanted them to go into the family business or be a doctor, a lawyer, or an architect. They feel that they're expected to do what their families have always wanted for them. Often financial security, outward respectability, or both are very important to these clients' parents, and those parents have communicated this to their children. Other clients have felt conflicted about having gone further than their working-class parents. They might be the first members of their families to go to university or find white-collar jobs, and now they might be under pressure from their parents for having turned their back on their roots. Still other clients feel the discontent of their parents for not having been successful enough. Some have star brothers and sisters and feel that they can never measure up, so why bother trying? Once these people are in this situation, they feel boxed in by conflicting pressures, and as a result, making change can be too difficult.

Other people tell themselves "If I make some changes at work, become successful, and make more money, then I'll be expected to take care of everyone, and my family responsibilities will be overwhelming!" or "If my business grows, will I have more paperwork to do? Goodness, I hate paperwork!" People are sometimes unconsciously afraid of what success will bring, and because of that fear, they sabotage their chances and essentially get in their own way. I know this may seem ridiculous and counter-productive, but it is an example of the quirky little tricks the mind and fear can play on us.

People who carry these feelings encounter a barrier that stops them from having the sorts of lives they really want. They feel that they're not good enough, but they want to please the people they care about whilst earning the respect of society. It's all very complicated.

Regret

As we get older we sometimes look at where we are now and wish we had done things differently in the past. We might say to ourselves "If only I had done another degree." or "If only I had gone into finance when I left school, I would not always be so worried about money." People often think it is too late to change things and therefore live in a perpetual state of regret. Living like this blocks our ability to give ourselves permission to do anything.

Mixed Messages

Many of my clients have grown up listening to real or perceived mixed messages. They have taken on broad messages like "Do well at school and work, but not as well as me", "You can do or have anything in life, but don't ever be selfish", or "It's important to be attractive to the opposite sex, but not *too* attractive or people will think you're loose."

Other clients haven't been provided with clear boundaries for many reasons. Because they don't always know what is allowed and what is not, they often think their situations to be unsafe. Understandably, this can result in a lot of confusion and insecurity, and often these anxieties persist well into adulthood.

Societal Constraints

Navigating our lives can be tremendously stressful. On top of the expectations those close to us may have for our decisions and behaviour, society's expectations have changed a lot in recent decades and are continuing to evolve at a dizzying rate. Whilst the world is undeniably easier in many ways, it is also more complicated and can be more difficult to navigate. Our roles as members of our communities and our families are less clear-cut than in previous times. Whereas people once lived in intensely social environments, modern societies today are filled with isolated individuals. Today, people often feel that they're being weak when they have to ask for help with their children or other responsibilities, when previously, collaboration was the norm. Many now feel that they are being judged as incapable when they show vulnerability.

In the past, people tended to be born into a particular social strata and culture and, from early on, basically knew how their lives would pan out. Today, most of us have a huge amount of freedom to choose where and how to live. That is a wonderful opportunity, but it is also a responsibility that can be quite overwhelming, as too much choice can be paralysing.

Many find themselves struggling to fill multiple roles at the same time: to be a successful businessperson, a full-time parent, a supportive partner, and a dutiful grown-up son or daughter. Unlike our ancestors, we don't always have a template to follow for how to behave in most situations.

So, for better or worse, we have to recognise that now more than ever, we're responsible for making the hard choices for our own lives. We're no longer funnelled through a set of criteria dictated by our socioeconomic backgrounds, educations, or cultures. We have to take on even more personal responsibility than we might have had to in the past, and therefore, it's even more important that we give ourselves permission to follow the path that is right for us.

Navel-Gazing

There are many derogatory (and sometimes quite humorous) terms used for people who look within and find answers from themselves or a higher power. Many people see working with a therapist/coach or being spiritual as signs of weakness. In fact, it recently came to someone's attention that I was working with a person considered to be quite successful in her field, and the first person was amazed and asked why the successful person needed a coach. This client was doing very well but wanted to do better. It dawned on me that many people think that only those who have problems or are not doing well seek professional help or try to better themselves. The common view is that only people in dire straits explore their own feelings and needs. This makes me incredibly sad, because people who think this way are missing out on a very rich world of knowledge and understanding of themselves, and in the vein of Louise Hay's succinct and pointed quote at the start of this chapter, awareness is fifty percent of growth. Without knowing yourself and how you work, how are you going to recognise what you want in life, and how are you going to figure out how to get it? If exploring your spirituality in some way, in accordance with any doctrine, is supportive and feels right then embrace those opportunities. Sometimes you might feel more comfortable keeping your practice private but, go ahead, navel-gaze, read touchy-feely literature, explore the woo-woo, talk with an angel or two if you like, and know that you can give yourself permission to explore what makes you tick; it will only help in the long run.

The Role of Personal Responsibility

—–~~◦◦◦◦◦◦◦◦~~–—

Man is condemned to be free; because once
thrown into the world, he is responsible for
everything he does. —Jean-Paul Sartre

—–~~◦◦◦◦◦◦◦◦~~–—

All too often, we blame others for why our lives have not turned out the way we would have wanted them to. Yes, others may have said or done something hurtful, rude, or even abusive, but we are the only ones who can control how that makes us feel, how it limits us, and how we allow those words or actions to dictate the rest of our lives.

Taking personal responsibility can often be difficult and painful, as it requires us to take a long, hard look at ourselves. This in no way means taking the blame for everything, but it does mean admitting our role in a situation or issue.

Like it or not, we are in charge of everything we feel, think, and do. We are responsible for how we interact with others, what we say, and the decisions we make for our lives. Recognising this is called taking personal responsibility, and unfortunately, it can sometimes be a hard pill to swallow.

In my personal and professional experience, when we come from a place of taking personal responsibility for our thoughts and actions, life becomes *much* easier. Personal responsibility is the stem of all empowerment.

Cleverly, we can all come up with many seemingly valid excuses to defer taking responsibility for ourselves. I once had a client who told me that he would never be able to make a success of his life because his father was so discouraging.

"He has never respected my achievements," my client explained. "He always puts me down."

When we talked through what was really going on, it became clear that the fact that his father was indeed discouraging had effectively given my client an excuse to not work as diligently as he could, push as hard as possible, and reach for the stars. On one level, he wanted all the success that, intellectually speaking, he knew he was capable of, but on another, he felt a degree of comfort in knowing that if his career didn't turn out as luminous as it might, he could always tell himself and everyone else that it was his father's fault for not being supportive. He could have been a big star in his field, *if only* Dad had been more generous with his support!

Baby Steps

——⁓⁓⊷⊶⊷⊶⁓⁓——

And no one will listen to us until we listen
to ourselves. —Marianne Williamson

——⁓⁓⊷⊶⊷⊶⁓⁓——

Fundamentally, as you will see, when you know you matter, you will give yourself permission to do whatever you feel is right for you. You have to allow yourself to think you can and need to do what you think is best for you. Recognising that you are worthwhile enough to care for yourself will lead to great things.

By practicing self-care and by nurturing your self-worth and self-confidence, you will start to become more comfortable with yourself and your aspirations, and be better able to lay the foundations for and construct your wonderful life. You will strengthen your trust in yourself and your power of intuition as well as your ability to assess situations realistically, regardless of how stressful they may be. This may involve dramatic or minuscule changes for you, but the result will be to give yourself permission to live in accordance with the real you.

Before you come out and declare your goals and ambitions and make big steps towards achieving them, you can explore everything you need to do for yourself in a very quiet way from within, at your own pace and in your own time. It's important that this exploration come before you make a big splash on the scene. In time, you will be able to do that bungee jump or climb that mountain. Ultimately, you will reach the great success or other achievement that you're working towards and can unveil it to others, but for now, it might be easier and safer to be on a covert mission!

Where Do We Go from Here?

For all the reasons discussed in this chapter, and more, many of us find it painfully difficult to give ourselves permission to change our lives for the better. The good news is that it doesn't have to be as laborious as we might think. You can start making real changes right now by giving yourself permission to explore what you need to do to be happy and free.

The chapters that follow will serve as a guide to understanding, identifying, and implementing the tools that will allow you to be comfortable with taking personal responsibility and giving yourself permission to make decisions that are in your best interest. This is *the Permission Journey*™.

Mostly, this book is about all the people out there who are far closer to realising their goals than they know. It is about you, it is about them, and, to some extent, it is also about me because I have lived through and continue to deal with issues related to letting myself be the person I need to be.

So, are changes of this sort achievable? Absolutely! Simple? Far more than you might think. Easy? Well, not necessarily. But then, we have just finished the first chapter. We have the rest of the book to discuss the steps you can take to start creating the life you have always wanted.

CHAPTER TWO

The Legacy of Childhood – My Story, Part One

Life's problems wouldn't be called "hurdles"
if there wasn't a way to get over them.
—Author Unknown

M y story, although colourful, is not one of violence and abject
horrors. As a therapist, I was trained never to tell anybody
anything about myself. However, I was also taught that in instances
when I think it might help the client, sharing my personal experiences
may be worthwhile. I have decided to be more open in this book than
I would be in a coaching or therapy session because I feel by doing
so it might help you, the reader. In the introduction, I mentioned that
I don't want to preach at you, I just want to be a guide. This chapter
describes my background, some low points, some high points and a
few adventures! I relate these occurrences as I experienced them at the
time, to set the scene as to how and why I got to a place where I put
myself last and didn't give myself permission to live my life. No matter

what happens in our lives I believe we can move past them and be happy from within. Chapter four goes on to tell of how I worked through the stages of the Permission Journey (outlined in chapter three) to attain both personal and professional freedom.

Family Tree

From the outside, my childhood looked idyllic. I was a pretty little girl; I was dressed in lovely, expensive dresses; and I was polite and well behaved. I'm told that my mother, father, other family members, nannies, friends, and just about everyone else doted on me. However, deep down, I was a very anxious child who would grow into an outwardly strong but inwardly weak and doubting woman. There seemed to be some chaos and much uncertainty in our family as I was growing up, and this atmosphere affected much of my life. I lived within an odd dichotomy: on the one hand, I was very independent because I had to be, but at the same time, I was very dependent on what people thought of me, and that dictated just about everything I did. Most of all, I cared deeply about whether my mother approved of what I did, thought, wore, said, and so on. By the time I was in my late twenties, I had done everything a girl from my socioeconomic background was supposed to do, and whilst I had some great and interesting experiences, I was not living an authentic life. I feel that this cost me, and others, dearly.

I was born to an American mother and Indian father. I grew up in London but spent most holidays in Los Angeles with my maternal grandparents. My grandfather was born in Chihuahua, Mexico. His family had been involved in the construction of the first railway between Mexico and the US. They knew Pancho Villa, the prominent Mexican general, and as they fled Mexico, he knew which train they were on and kept his revolutionaries from attacking it. My grandfather studied as a lawyer and engineer. He worked for Hughes Aircrafts after World War II and then started his own engineering firm in Los Angeles, where he often won interesting and sensitive government aerospace contracts. Although very smart and often quite supportive, he would sometimes give with one hand and take away with the other, which sent us all mixed messages.

My grandmother grew up in a difficult family, with an abusive father, and from the age of fourteen she worked to support her mother and sister. At fifteen she became a dancer and performed on cruise ships all over the world and in the grand spectacles that were Depression-era movies. After marrying my grandfather, having barely finished high school and without a college degree, she became the first female chairman of the Board of Education for the Los Angeles Unified School District. She then worked on my grandfather's government contracts, and in the oven in our kitchen – an oven we still have – she built and tested some of the components that guided Apollo 11 to the moon. She was quite self-assured, and she and I had a special bond. I loved and respected her deeply and she had a huge influence on my life.

My mother, an only child, was and still is blonde and gorgeous. She looked like a movie star to me when I was growing up: she was incredibly chic and lived a glamorous life to match. However, she found life with her driven parents quite difficult and constantly felt criticised and unloved. She moved to London because she had seen the film La Dolce Vita and thought that she would find a version of it there. My parents met through friends when my mother was travelling in Europe. She was twenty-five years younger than my father, a dashing international businessman originally from India who had successfully assimilated into Western culture.

My father and mother travelled the world for his work, and since my sister, Heera, and I had nannies we were often able to travel with them. School holidays with our grandparents in Los Angeles were wonderful. Life was quite structured there: dinner was always served at six, and my grandmother would summon us by ringing the triangle in the garden. We celebrated fantastic Christmases together, and I was lucky enough to have a birthday during the summer, so we were always all together then.

Heera and I had few toys because we travelled so much and it was difficult to carry everything around. The result was that I treasured the toys I did have and was able to really exercise my creativity with them. I invented loads of versions of a single board game, and I was a huge fan of dressing up in whatever I could find in my mother's wardrobe. She had lovely clothes, and she didn't mind if I played with them as long as I was careful and put them back properly.

Smoke and Mirrors

When I was eight, we moved to a very big house in the middle of London. Things were seemingly good in the early years, but there was always an underlying sense of confusion or unpredictability. My father was often away, either on business or in the hospital. He seemed to have a lot of health problems, although it wasn't completely clear to me what was actually wrong with him.

I remember my father invariably dressing very formally. He nearly always wore a three-piece suit with a collared shirt and a tie. For casual wear, he would exchange the suit jacket and waistcoat for a cashmere sweater, and I marvelled at the softness of it. When my father *was* at home, I went into my parents' room in the morning and was always comforted to see my father in his paisley pyjamas, as they meant that he was going to stay for a while instead of rushing away again. I loved him and wanted to spend more time with him, but the opportunity just was not there. I would put my party dress on when my father came home because I was so happy to see him and wanted to make him happy too. I cherished the times when he did take me – just me – out. One day when I had a cold, he took me to dinner and ordered very hot Indian food to clear out my head. It worked.

My mother loved my sister and me very much, and if we broke something, she wouldn't get angry with us, because she knew we didn't do it on purpose. We were very good girls. But I knew I had to behave or my mother would get upset, and that was the last thing I wanted in the world. Although she's American, my mother had taken on board a lot of English ideas about social class and proper behaviour. I dressed the way my mother thought I should dress, which never really seemed quite me. I wanted my mother to be pleased with me all the time. I think this came from the fact that she had high standards and demanded quite a bit of people. At the same time, I put unrealistic expectations on myself to be perfect. I worried about what my mother and other people thought of me and did not think about what I wanted for myself. As children, we learn from what we see and feel around us. We observe our parents and other adults interacting with the world, and based on that, we draw conclusions and usually emulate those interactions.

When I was twelve my father left us. As devastating as it was for me to learn, it must have been worse for my mother. My sister and I were told that we would not see him anymore. After this shock, my mother's emotional reliance on me escalated and my almost pathological need to keep her happy really overtook me. I didn't want to do anything that would upset her. Maybe I felt she had too much on her plate, maybe I wanted to protect her, maybe I also felt that it would just be easier for me to carry the burden, but the pressure to do the right thing all the time kicked into high gear. I felt incredible loyalty to my mother, and she was very appreciative of the support.

Growing up, I felt that being different and having my own thoughts and values were of no benefit to me. I felt that I could not be myself and that I had to do and say all the right things to stay under the radar. I sensed

I couldn't tell anyone how I truly felt or ask for help if I really needed it for fear of upsetting the apple cart.

Sleeping on Couches

As I entered my teenage years, I tried to express myself a little more. The 1980s were a great time to be young in London. The New Romantics and glam pop were popular, and young people felt free to be expressive and creative. My friends and I loved shopping for cool ensembles at all the mod markets around London. We bought fun outfits for next to nothing and had a great time wearing them. It all seemed very innocent; most of us didn't get involved in drugs, drink to excess, or sleep around, but we did go to the pub, go out dancing and have parties.

During this time funds were really low and it was often difficult to pay the utility bills. My mother was determined to keep the house. After all, it was our home. She ultimately took in up to six lodgers to help financially. She liked to keep busy and keep her mind off of things by having people in the house. It was usually filled with an endless cast of characters in the form of party guests, visitors, and lodgers. They brought with them all sorts of colourful lives. One lodger said he was a bishop in the Church of England. He showed us his vestments and many beautiful gold crosses and rings, but it soon became evident that he was a male prostitute trolling the streets of Mayfair for clients. One day he just disappeared, having cut some electrical wires and making off with anything he could, including the phones, radios, the iron, and even the ironing board!

My first encounter with paranoid schizophrenia came in the form of a forty-five-year-old woman who came very close to pushing me out of my seventh-floor bedroom window! Another lodger had invited her into the house in the middle of the night when my mother was away.

One of my saving graces was that I loved school, which offered security, friends, and a regular meal every day. I loved the fact that I had a timetable and knew where I was supposed to be every minute of the day – luxury! I also felt I could mostly be myself there. Thankfully, since money was really tight, our schools put us on scholarships but academically I was average.

I remember with great fondness the fun and camaraderie my best friend, Kate, and I had rowing on the Serpentine whilst revising for our history exam. Usually, she rowed whilst I asked the questions, because otherwise I generally ended up dropping an oar in the water. She would bring me to her house to eat and stay over. Her parents went to great lengths to include me, and their home provided me with a wonderfully secure environment. With no idea of how confused things were in my household, my friend's family did not fuss over me; they just shared their Sunday lunch and showed me what an ordinary family looked like. I really enjoyed the reliability and stability that school and friends offered me.

Eventually we lost our house. I was at school that day, and I was called to the office and told to go home. My mother had been informed that she had a few hours to take as many of our personal things as possible out of the house. She hired a moving company, which stole a lot of our stuff, and she had piled whatever was left into and on top of our Mini. I arrived home as the moving van was pulling away and the bailiffs were locking the door. My mother, Heera, and I sat on the pavement next to the comically laden car wondering what to do next. We were never allowed into our house again.

We ended up staying with a friend of my mother's, who was very much a 'bon viveur'. He had a eccentric flat in affluent Belgravia, and my sister and I waited until the day's party was over before we could go to sleep on the sofa amongst half-filled champagne glasses, overflowing ashtrays, and rotting flowers. Thankfully, in time, my grandparents helped us get a new house.

Needless to say, I learned about resilience and independence, including how to take care of myself.

Goodbye

One evening, nearly two years later, when I was sixteen, a family friend rang the house, and I answered the phone.

"Did your father die?" he asked abruptly.

"Um, not as far as I know," I said. "Why?"

"Well, it says in *The Times* obituary column that someone with the same name as your father died in Surrey a few days ago."

"Well, that would probably be my father."

The man quickly hung up. Our lodger's French boyfriend had just come to visit, and after I made a few calls, to no avail, I asked him to call my father's house. I had not rung my father for years, but I could still remember his number. I told the boyfriend to ask for my father. He did, paused, thanked whomever was on the other end of the line, hung up, turned to me, and asked me what "passed away" meant.

That was how I learned that my father had died. I had not seen him for four years.

When my mother came home, I told her what had happened. It was hard for her, and it was hard for me too. I became depressed and worried that my father had not gone to Heaven, which was a terribly upsetting thought. At school, I had taken Religious Studies and was intrigued and comforted by the thought of a higher power. In typical Priya-fashion, I decided that *I* was solely responsible for getting my father to Heaven. I put a picture of him by my bed and prayed for him every night, begging God to let him in.

My room seemed to be abnormally cold, and I became more and more depressed until one day my dear friend Crispin broke into the house. He came into my room, tore off the sheets, and said, "That's it. I am getting you out of here." I am eternally grateful to him for rescuing me from the dark place I had fallen into.

At that point, I realised that the responsibility for my father's salvation was becoming a very heavy burden to bear. For some reason I felt that I had to bargain with God and save him, when it really was not my job at all! I picked up the photograph of my father, looked at it, and told him that I was letting him go and that he would be on his own from now on. I then put the picture away face down in a drawer. In this instance I recognised where my responsibilities truly lay – and where they did not.

However, I refocused and redoubled my efforts in taking care of my mother. Since childhood, I tried really hard to make things easier for her, to be there for her, and to help pick up the pieces when problems arose. I had also learned to anticipate when problems would come down the pipeline. I did all I could to avert any huge mishaps and mitigate collateral damage when something slipped through the cracks.

Eventually, both my mother and sister moved to Los Angeles, so I lived alone in the house for my last year of school. I had very little money, but we had scraped by before by taking in lodgers, so I decided to get one. His name was Tintin. He was about twenty, was very cool and everyone knew him, so I gained instant street cred amongst my friends. He was a night owl, so we usually had breakfast together, after which I would go to school all day whilst he slept. He would get up just in time to make me dinner most evenings, and then he would go out and I would go to sleep. I will never forget his kindness and friendship either.

Time for Change

I did reasonably well at school, although perhaps not as well as I might have done had things been easier. Somehow, I was admitted to Warwick University in the UK. I had never seen the university before I arrived at my housing.

At the time, I was one of a handful of students at Warwick who had been to private school, and because of that, I felt that people did not like me much. I was also taking a course that didn't suit me very well, so after two years, I transferred to the University of Southern California (USC). My grandparents helped with tuition, and I received grants and loans to cover the rest.

I really enjoyed being at USC and closer to my family. In my senior year, I met my future husband. We were introduced at a fraternity party because neither of us drank alcohol. I didn't like the taste and also dreaded the thought of being out of control.

Charmed Life

When my future husband and I met, he was recovering from an accident. It was a difficult time in his life. I think that we were brought together because we both needed the support, love, and care we could provide for each other. I liked the fact that he provided security; he was wonderfully solid and reliable. I knew exactly what was going to happen every day. We moved in with each other after we graduated from university and were engaged a few years later.

One morning just before we were married, I woke up with double vision. As I was working as a graphic designer at the time, this was a real problem, added to the fact that because I lived in LA, I invariably needed to drive a lot to get anywhere. I went to a few ophthalmologists who tried various unsuccessful treatments. Nobody suggested seeing a neuro-opthalmologist. Three weeks later, I woke up with clear vision. The condition seemed to have disappeared as quickly as it had started. Then, a year later, I started to experience the sensation of electric currents going up and down my legs. It felt odd but I didn't pay much attention to it. Just like the double vision, it disappeared a few weeks later.

As an anxious person, I was stressed about organising our wedding ceremony and the party afterwards. Everything had to be absolutely perfect (subsequently, I have learned to move away from a need for perfection). Originally, I had suggested to my fiancé and my mother that we elope to avoid what I knew was going to be a whirlwind of activity. They were both horrified and assured me that they would help organise everything. Somehow, it didn't work out that way, mostly because I didn't let them and insisted on doing almost everything myself.

I became more and more worried about what everyone would think of our wedding, about adhering to the rules of traditional etiquette, and about doing everything just right so my mother and society would approve. The planning seemed to take on a life of its own, and just like Jack in "Chapter One: Why We Don't Give OurSelves Permission", I found myself being whisked along by that big, heavy freight train. It felt like it was tearing ahead so quickly that I wouldn't have been able to slow it down or stop it even if I had wanted to.

Looking back, I can see clearly that at this time, I had lost my sense of self. Even though I was preparing for my wedding, I was living for others. I worried a lot about my place in the world, whether I was doing things the right way, and what people would think.

The day of the wedding eventually came. Bridesmaids, family, and great friends came to Los Angeles for the celebration. Friendship and love were everywhere. And yet, the night before the wedding, after the rehearsal dinner, I drove back to my hotel all alone. At the time, I felt slightly put out and felt that no one cared about me, but I now see that I had taken absolute control of everything and hadn't allowed anyone in. It seemed easier for me to be alone and in complete control than to enjoy my friends and family. This was further evident the following day when I found *myself* driving the minivan containing all the bridesmaids and their dresses to the church!

The wedding had the usual dramas that many do – my drunken godmother lurching at my mother but hitting the priest instead as he stepped in to protect her, one of the groomsmen offering my godson pot, my sister hijacking the limousine with the rest of the wedding party for a joyride around LA as my husband and I waited for everyone at the reception – but, despite it all, we had a lovely day.

Two days later, we left for our much-anticipated honeymoon in Egypt. When we arrived in Frankfurt for our connecting flight, we were met by a film crew who asked me, and some of the other passengers, if we were afraid to travel. Apparently there had been a bombing in Cairo. As I had grown up in London at the height of the IRA campaign, I wasn't overly concerned and insisted that my husband and I continue our trip. On arrival in Egypt, we found out that it had not been a bombing at all but the massacre of a large number of tourists in Luxor by a terrorist group. Still, I was not dissuaded.

The Tipping Point

When I awoke on our first day in Cairo, I found that I had pins and needles in my left hand. As the trip continued, the feeling spread along my whole left side. Eventually, I was barely able to walk. Because of the problems in Egypt, most of the flights in and out of the country were grounded, but we managed to get one of the few planes back to the United States.

On arrival, I was taken straight to the hospital for a scan. When the results came back, the doctor told me that there was good news and bad news. The good news was that I didn't have a tumour in my brain, but the bad news was that there was something wrong and that I would have to be admitted for more tests the next day. I wasn't allowed to eat, shower, or change my clothes. I was smelly, hungry, and tired after all that travelling. I remember lying in a cold, hard hospital bed, exhausted and scared. My mother and my husband had gone home because I had told them to. I felt I had to be in control and couldn't show my family any weakness. I worried that everyone at the hospital was angry with me because it was Thanksgiving Day and I had ruined the holiday. It was all too much and I started to cry, but I will be forever grateful to the nurse who came in, held my hand, and comforted me.

My husband was very supportive. He cut my food, brought me to doctor appointments, and did all he could to help. At one stage, I had to go to the hospital to have a lumbar puncture. I remember lying on my side on an exam bed staring at the wall whilst the neurologist tried to insert the needle into my spine. Finally, the doctor said that it wasn't working and that I might have to go to radiology instead but that he would try one more time. I thought, "I can't do it. That's another three hours of waiting." Then, I thought, "God, if you exist, now is the time. On the count of three please." I counted silently, and on three, the doctor said, "I got it!" From then on, I have never doubted that there is a higher power and that he/she/it is there to support me – especially when I'm open and when I ask for help.

For two years, I had MRI scans every six months. I really didn't do much research or think about my condition until May 1999, when the results of an MRI showed disease progression and I was formally diagnosed with MS. Because it had gone on for so long, and I was feeling fine, and earlier tests had shown only a slight chance of MS, I didn't expect to hear that actual diagnosis and was quite shocked by it. As the MRIs and their results had become so routine over past the two years, my husband wasn't with me when I received the news, and afterwards, I did what any Kapoor would do: I carried on and honoured a lunch plan I had with a work colleague as though nothing had happened. It always takes a few hours or even days for things to sink in for me.

This started the long journey of healing both physically and emotionally, years of medication, tests, pain, uncertainty, much learning, and many blessings.

It used to be when I read or heard people say that they considered getting an illness to be a blessing in disguise, I would think they were crazy. How could they say that? But now I understand. The MS diagnosis made me stop and take a look at what I was doing to myself. It was a tipping point in my life, and I am grateful for it. Given this experience, my wish now is to help others find a way to change tack much sooner than I did, before they sail into the storm of a chronic illness or worse. Read on, and we will navigate the seven seas to freedom together.

CHAPTER THREE

The Permission Journey

—————wvoooeoooeooovw—————

We either make ourselves miserable, or we make
ourselves strong. The amount of work is the same.
—Carlos Castaneda

—————wvoooeoooeooovw—————

The ultimate purpose of this book is to give you the space, desire, and tools to give yourself permission to live *your* life.

Giving yourself permission means allowing yourself to think and do what you think is best for yourself. People consistently balk at this comment. Many of my clients say, "I can't just think of myself; I have my children to worry about," or "It's not all about me; my parents would be so disappointed." They often worry that they'll be seen as selfish and often truly believe that they are being self-centred.

I would like to challenge that thinking. When you go on a plane and the safety announcement says that in case of emergency, you should put on your oxygen mask before helping others. Why do you think they say that?

Imagine a scenario in which a mother sees her oxygen mask drop in front of her face and knows that the flight attendant has instructed her to put hers on first. Instead, she looks over at her small child and decides to reach for his first. He is vulnerable; he needs her help. She takes the time to unbuckle her belt and reach over. Her son is upset and reaching for her, squirming in his seat. She has to tussle with him before she can pull down his oxygen mask, and doing so has taken a lot of time; too much, in fact. The grim reality is that she could pass out due to lack of oxygen and become incapable of helping him put his mask on. Even if the child is still conscious, he probably isn't able to reach the mask and doesn't even know what to do with it. They may both die, utterly needlessly.

This depressing analogy highlights that it is imperative for you to take care of yourself before helping others, for their sake as much as yours. And that means allowing yourself to figure out what *taking care of yourself* means. When we take care of ourselves, we make ourselves strong enough to take care of others.

Trains, Planes, and Automobiles

To illustrate the process outlined in the book of giving yourself permission to ultimately live your life I am going to use the analogy of a journey around the world. Sometimes we need help and time to get to the place where we can truly give ourselves permission to live our lives the way we want to. These are stages of the Permission Journey (see Figure 3:1).

I have chosen an island group from each of the seven oceans of the world as stops. The journey starts as you travel from your own home, wherever you are in the world, to your first destination, the sun-drenched

Hawaiian Islands in the North Pacific. As you travel this stage you read, assimilate the concepts and process the information of "Chapter Five: Give YourSelf Permission to Know You Matter." That's stage 1 of the Permission Journey. Chapters 5-12 are each an individual stage. This can take as long as you need, as can any stage of the journey. If you're taking your time, you might chose to take a slow cruise ship; sometimes you may be able to travel faster by taking a plane; other times you may hop on a train, drive a car, or ride a bicycle; or you may take the slowest but often most deliberate method of all and walk. The point is, you get to choose how you navigate each stage, with the intention of reaching each destination having mastered the concept and hence knowing the route very well. You can then apply what you've learned in that stage to the next stage, and so on. It is an incremental process. Without understanding and travelling through each stage, you are not going to be able to move forward on your round-the-world trip.

So now let's move through the rest of the stages of your journey. The examples I give are only that; please feel free to pick seven locations for yourself and chart your own course. Remember, it's how you travel through the stages that matter. Visiting the inspiring sites en route and your arrival are your rewards. Now it's time to embark on the rest of your journey by setting off for the warm waters of the Society Islands in the South Pacific. You'll then move on to the home of over ten million chinstrap penguins, the Sandwich Islands in the South Atlantic, then to the striking volcanic Canary Islands in the North Atlantic, to the historic Franz Josef Land archipelago in the Arctic, and then on to a lovely stay in the sandy Maldives in the Indian Ocean. Your last stop before going home is the ecologically rich Balleny Islands in the Southern Ocean. After you've given yourself permission to visit all these great places and have learned the tools and started to apply them, it's time to go home with all this newfound personal empowerment and to see how you can integrate it into everyday life. As you travel this last stage home, you'll go through the important process of *giving yourself permission to dream big and live* your *life*. This last stage has no recognisable islands or ocean destination, as you are to end up back where you started. It just might look different now that you know and care about yourself and you might also have new dreams for how it looks.

Every time you reach a destination, you'll have the opportunity to take time to reflect a little on your journey and decide what souvenirs in the form of lessons learned you want to take with you and which items in the form of unhealthy thoughts, memories, or behaviours you want to leave behind, therefore lightening the load in your suitcase.

The Permission Journey map (Figure 3:1) illustrates the following destinations:

Stage 1: GYS Permission to Know You Matter
Stage 2: GYS Permission to Know What You Care About
Stage 3: GYS Permission to Take Back Your Life
Stage 4: GYS Permission to Be Brave
Stage 5: GYS Permission to Be Happy
Stage 6: GYS Permission to Have Healthy Relationships
Stage 7: GYS Permission to Know Your Dream Team
Homeward Stage: GYS Permission to Dream Big and Live *Your* life

You might find you have more experience with a specific stage or that one may be easier to navigate than another. Again, it is an individual process, and depending on your personality and experience, you'll find some journeys more difficult than others.

I'll briefly outline the specifics of each stage of the Permission Journey here and then return to the story of how I travelled though it and eventually came out the other end. However, there is always more to learn and experience. What we learn from our experiences and what we implement in our lives is completely within our control. We have the ability to create the lives we want.

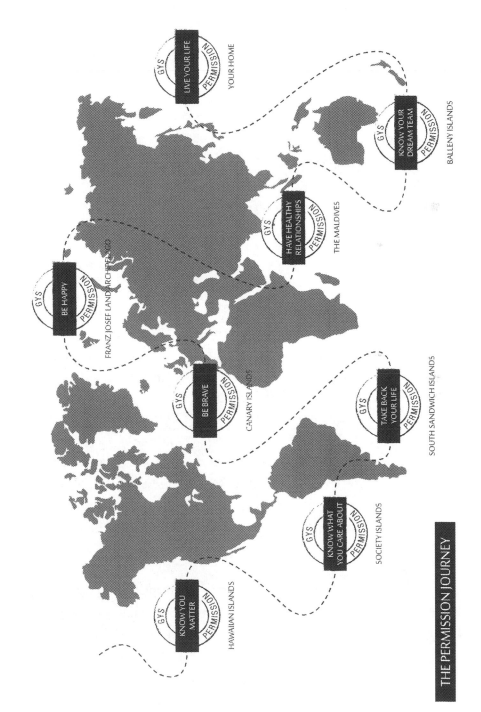

Figure 3:1: The Permission Journey

Give YourSelf Permission to Know You Matter is the self-esteem and confidence stage. Here we will look at how to take care of yourself and start believing that you are really worth it. You'll be taken through the "Knowing You Matter Pathway" and you will learn how to pay attention to how you physically feel and what your body is trying to tell you.

In **Give YourSelf Permission to Know What You Care About,** we will explore what values are specifically and how living by them can only help you in the long run. You'll also do quite a bit of exploration of how to unearth those sometimes elusive qualities. Once your values are solidified, you'll look at practical ways to use them.

We will then proceed to **Give YourSelf Permission to Take Back Your Life**. Here, you'll explore why taking personal responsibility will benefit you, along with concepts and tools for how to fully grasp the reality that you are completely in charge of everything you do, feel, think, and say. Yes, others can place pressure on your decision-making, but ultimately, only you have control over how you react to such influences.

Next, we will address ways to **Give YourSelf Permission to be Brave**. You'll look at the role fear plays in your life and how you can overcome limiting thoughts. You'll look at how fears are sometimes valid and sometimes not and how to discern between the two. You'll also take a look at how you can learn to trust yourself and others and how the quality of resilience is an integral component of checking the reality of who you really are and what is really going on.

The next stage involves how to **Give YourSelf Permission to be Happy**. It might seem surprising, but a lot of people feel guilty about being happy or don't know how to be happy or to flip that switch to having a positive mindset. Here, we will look at some of the most useful and widely used techniques of positive psychology.

Since humans are innately social beings, we will proceed to consider how you can **Give YourSelf Permission to Have Healthy Relationships**. Using the knowledge and insight you've gained up to this point, you'll explore how to interact with others, regardless of what they do.

Give YourSelf Permission to Know Your Dream Team will look at how to identify, be grateful for, and be accountable to the people in your life who have believed in you in the past and continue to help in important ways. *Dream Team* may be an overused term, but you'll see how important and beneficial it is to honour these relationships. You will also look at how you can be on other people's Dream Teams, on your own terms, because you want to, and without losing yourself in the process.

Penultimately, we will embrace how to **Give YourSelf Permission to Dream Big**. This can be very difficult for some people. Really, dreaming big is the springboard to achieving everything you want for and from your life. This starts with dreaming quietly but planning big. It's about giving yourself permission to explore any possibility you choose to live the life you want, one which is in sync with who you are, what you value, and who you authentically want to be.

Finally, the ultimate goal in the second half of this journey is to **Give YourSelf Permission to Live *Your* Life,** the stage at which you can explore and participate in all the great whizz-bang, show-the-world empowerment self-help programs and literature out there.

Exercise: Give YourSelf Permission to Figure Out What You Want from Your Life

Take a few minutes to ask yourself what you would like to have given yourself permission to do by the end of this book, and write a list in the present tense. This could contain almost anything.

When I asked myself the same question, I came up with a long list covering three full pages and including statements like, "I give myself permission to have fun," "I give myself permission to be a good sleeper," "I give myself permission to be an inspired speaker," and even more excitingly, "I give myself permission to meet loads of great people through my work."

Don't worry if this seems out of reach at the moment; you can revisit this exercise at any time. But, if you have a list you like, consider keeping a copy of it in your phone, on your computer, or even stuck inside the door of your medicine cabinet – somewhere private where you can see it and remind yourself why you're so committed to making changes that are good for you.

CHAPTER FOUR

Giving Myself Permission – My Story, Part Two

—⁓⦵⦵⦵⦵⦵⦵⁓—

When we have begun to take charge of our
lives, to own ourselves, there is no longer any
need to ask permission of someone.
—George O'Neil

—⁓⦵⦵⦵⦵⦵⦵⁓—

Taking Back My Life

Oddly, or fortunately, the MS diagnosis gave me permission to start taking care of myself and honouring what I did and did not want to do or be. However, it took me a very long time to get to a place where I was really able to listen to myself, honour my needs, and live a whole life.

Quite quickly, I was able to say, "I need to take things easy today because tomorrow is important and I have to be healthy and well." It became easier for me to say no than it had ever been before I became ill, because I felt I had an excuse to take care of myself. I still worried that I was being selfish or unkind, but it was alright to think of myself and my physical and psychological needs, as I could hide behind my illness. I had to create boundaries, but before that, I had to understand what would and would not work for me. I also had to come to terms with the realisation that I couldn't make everyone happy all the time. I needed to learn to choose my battles. I had to learn to make hard choices and be willing to change. This was all in an effort just to survive.

I went back to work part-time after the honeymoon, and it was difficult. After about a year, I left my position. In hindsight, I should have stayed; I loved my job, and it would have kept me engaged with others. Instead, I started my own graphic design business and got heavily involved with a women's service organisation doing charity work in the Los Angeles area. Slowly, I sought complementary therapies to Western medicine. I pursued relaxation techniques, guided imagery, aromatherapy, exercise and nutrition, and I saw a psychotherapist. In an attempt to eliminate all the stress from my life, I withdrew a little from my mother, and just about everyone else. However, I still felt incredibly guilty about not doing what I thought was as much as she would have wanted or liked. Whilst I was trying to nurture myself and my health, I was only really addressing the surface issues and was hiding from everything else.

Stumbling upon My Purpose

A few years after I was diagnosed, my eyesight started to go south. My eyes are my weak link. I had developed nerve damage from the first few bouts of optic neuritis, six-nerve palsy, and nystagmus. It was getting more and more difficult to see the computer screen, so I could no longer do any graphic design work.

After years of working relatively successfully with a combination of traditional and complementary medicines, I decided I wanted to start a holistic wellness centre for people with chronic illness. I realised that

I would need some letters behind my name to legitimise myself to any donors. After a little research, I settled on the master's program in Marriage and Family Therapy at my undergraduate alma mater, USC. I had been seeing a therapist, and it had been helping, but I by no means thought that that line of work was going to be part of my life's purpose. As I looked at the application for admission, I realised to my horror that I had to take the Graduate Record Exam, which had a maths component. I hadn't seen a maths problem for over fifteen years!

I worked diligently with a tutor to learn algebra, calculus, and even division all over again. I had an additional problem: the test had to be taken on a computer, and no paper version was available. The screens they made us use at the testing centre were very, very old and difficult to read, but I battled through. As the test progressed, candidates were given more difficult questions if they were doing well. Halfway through one of the maths components I got a tricky question and knew I was doing well. I looked up at the heavens and thanked God for his help. This was the second time in my life I recognised and knew without a doubt that I was not alone. On completion, I was automatically given my score – I got the exact score I needed to be admitted into the program, not a point higher or lower. I took this as a sign that I was supposed to do this course and that I was on the right path. However, I could barely focus for hours after the exam. All I could see was a kaleidoscope of amazing colours, shapes, and sparkles. Although it was quite pretty, it was slightly unnerving.

The program I attended was academically rigorous and there was a lot of reading. Because of my eyes, this was slow going for me. I had also started some very strong MS progression–slowing medication, essentially low-grade chemotherapy, and I got quite good at giving myself the injections, but the side effects were really debilitating. I had flu-like symptoms for at least a day after each dose. I could barely get out of bed. However, I did not have one MS relapse for the ten years I was on it.

As part of my degree, I was invited to do research with one of the leaders in the field of Clinical Psychology and Ageing. Her lab was one of the most selective and sought after for doctoral candidates worldwide, and it was a huge honour to be included as a master's student. I collaborated with one of her best PhD students on an Alzheimer's project. I worked hard and learned so much. I will always be grateful to Poorni because she believed in me, trusted me, and fought for me to be listed as one of the authors on the published study.

I remember feeling very humble because I was the lowest person on the rung in the research team and everyone else was so brilliant. At school I had been told that I was quite an average performer, so I felt almost as though I had tricked someone to get into the lab. What was *I* doing there? I felt like a fraud, but I now know that this thinking was purely self-sabotage.

I loved the program and the therapy work I did. I had great supervisors, learned a lot, and was doing well. All of a sudden I realised that this was what I was meant to do in life, and it felt natural and great!

When I graduated, I interned at a neurology clinic providing therapy to patients with neurological impairments such as Parkinson's, epilepsy, and stroke. In a funny way, working in a neurology clinic was the best place for me. Going into the record room where there were hundreds and hundreds of patient files, I started to think that everyone in the world had a neurological disorder and that I was lucky to have MS. I felt that it was probably the best of a difficult lot. I was grateful that I didn't have dystonia, Tourette's, or Alzheimer's! I also realised that I had so far escaped relatively easily, because most of the people I worked with were suffering from worse symptoms than I. However, people with MS or any chronic illness live with varying degrees of severity. Our conditions are all relative, and we all have different burdens and trials to bear. It is a very individual process, I just considered myself lucky given the situation I was in at the time.

In a very odd way, being a therapist suited me extremely well because it was all about the other person. For better or worse, this was something I knew well. I had made my life all about other people and had completely negated myself along the way. Whilst I was working very well with clients, I still didn't feel like I was worthy of giving myself permission to live the life I felt I needed to live. I had become my own worst enemy, never prioritising my own needs and interests and assuming chores and responsibilities that weren't really mine.

I began to develop and strengthen my intuition. At first it would give me insight into what a client needed, but I was tentative and sometimes did little with the information. I doubted myself, but in time, I started to listen to my intuition and act upon it.

Moving Away

My husband was very supportive of me, and I of him. We had a good life and a lovely house in a beach community near Los Angeles. It was different from London, but it was safe, comfortable, clean, and easy living. But something wasn't working.

As time went on, my husband and I were growing further and further apart. We separated, moved apart, and got back together four times before we finally called it quits. We went to couples therapy and tried everything we could think of. It was immensely sad, as we really cared for each other and had supported each other through so much. The whole process was incredibly difficult. Maybe we had married too young, before we really knew what we wanted for our lives, and we just grew into different people with different needs, likes, and wants. I never quite know what to say when people ask me, "What happened? Why did you get divorced?" It happened, it was painful and it took me years to recover from it. I wouldn't change anything from my time with him, and I have absolutely no regrets.

On the Ledge

Aged thirty-seven, I decided that it would be sensible to have my eggs frozen in case I thought I might want my own child one day. I didn't want to rush into meeting someone new and getting married just because my biological clock was ticking. I also thought it would appease my family and others who thought it would be a shame for me not to have children.

I am highly sensitive to medication and neither my doctors nor I could have anticipated the trouble I would have with the hormone therapy required for this process. A bad reaction, caused by the interactions of various other medications combined with the emotions related to the difficulties I had been having in my personal life, resulted in a disastrous outcome. Essentially, it was a perfect storm. I became almost psychotic, and at one point I came very close to jumping off the ledge of my twelfth-floor downtown loft. I remember looking out over the city. All the bright twinkling lights were so mesmerising. They pulsed hypnotically and were almost beckoning me. It seemed very peaceful … and then all of a sudden I had a flash of lucidity. I realised what I was about to do, and I was really afraid.

"Priya," I told myself, "this is the *last* thing you should do. You are a therapist. What kind of message are you giving your patients if you leave them this way?"

As a therapist, I knew all about how medication, stress, and depression can affect people. I suddenly realised that the person who wanted to take her own life was not the real me. For a moment, I could see and hear the monster inside me, which often told me that I was useless and stupid and that nothing good was ever going to happen for me. I recognised *it* as the cause of much of my self-sabotaging behaviour.

All my life I had lived according to what I thought other people needed and wanted from me. Ironically, this is what saved me now. I found strength in the knowledge that my patients needed me, but more importantly, it would have been very harmful to them if I had jumped off the ledge. I was accountable to them.

I often hear people talk of how selfish people who commit suicide are. How could they do that to their families? Having come close to doing that myself, I know that the thought of family and friends rarely crosses the distressed person's mind. They are in pain, and they simply want to get out of a situation that has become unbearable. I was just lucky to have my education, awareness, strength, and that very brief, clear whisper.

During that moment of clarity, I knew I needed help. At 10 p.m. I called my neurologist, who happened to work at the same clinic as I. Both literally and figuratively, he talked me down from the ledge. I will be eternally grateful to him.

Taking Personal Responsibility

———ᘛᑋᴗⱺᘒᴖⱺⱺᑋᘒⱺⱺᴖᴗ———

Accept who you are; and revel in it.
—Mitch Albom, *Tuesday with Morrie*

———ᘛᑋᴗⱺᘒᴖⱺⱺᑋᘒⱺⱺᴖᴗ———

When I finally accepted that things were just not working out for me, I started to explore what was holding me back from achieving the life I wanted. I realised that it was not other people who were getting in my way or that I lived with a chronic illness; it was me! Not my mother, nor the legacy of my father or anybody else, just me. My own decisions, interpretations, and perceptions were getting in my way. *I* was the one who had decided that I would sacrifice my own preferences and interests in order to do what I thought everyone else wanted. *I* was the one who was running around in circles trying to keep everyone else in my life happy. I had discounted and failed to honour what I really wanted from my life. In short, I was not taking personal responsibility for my life, thoughts, needs, desires, and well-being. I was letting others dictate what I should do – or, in truth, my *perception* of what they wanted me to do.

I had challenged my mother when our opinions clashed rather than accepting that she had one way of seeing things and I had another. I thought that she would be disappointed in me if I did what I wanted or that the choices I wanted to make were not ones she would approve of. It took a while before I understood that I didn't have to first consider how I thought my mother would react before doing anything for myself. I had never learned how to give myself permission to wholly trust myself, to see my own opinions as primary.

Over time, I learned that I could give myself permission to present myself to the world the way I wanted, to disagree with my mother about fundamental issues without feeling hurt or upset, to understand that we were both entitled to our own views and to live accordingly. Ultimately, I learned, if I wanted things to change, I already had the power to effect that change. I could decide to let the other people in my life be themselves, and to give myself the same freedom to take responsibility for my decisions and myself.

Whether the people in my life were actually judging me or not, I needed to reach the point at which I could stop judging myself according to how I perceived others viewed me.

Spreading My Wings

When you have been with the same person for over fifteen years, you realise that most of your pictures are of the two of you together. Each event or moment in time has the potential to stir up all sorts of memories of the relationship, the joy and the sadness. As a result, you end up displaying pictures from bygone days, of fun events in childhood or teenage larks. I found my class photo from when I was fifteen and put it up in my new flat. Since I was so happy at school and was still friends with quite a few girls in the image, I felt safe and comfortable looking at it.

Quite by chance, when my friend Alec looked at the picture, he asked me, "Knowing what you know now, what would you tell that fifteen-year-old girl?"

Without skipping a beat, I turned to him and said, "I would probably tell her never to leave London."

In that moment I realised with startling clarity that, objectively, nothing was tying me to the United States and that I could leave whenever I wanted. Alec's simple question had given me permission to listen to myself.

After many years of living and working in Los Angeles, I reached a point at which I knew that the right thing for me was to make a move. I had already worked on changing my role in my mother's life and subsequently in my grandmother's. I understood that over the course of my time in Los Angeles, I had assumed responsibility for everyone else. I had felt that I could never leave Los Angeles because my family needed me. I became resentful of and angry with them at times and experienced the role of a victim, of someone who sacrificed her own happiness and well-being for the welfare of others. But the truth of the matter was that I had chosen everything in my life and that nobody else was really making me do anything, even though it felt like it at the time. I was the one who had decided to stay in Los Angeles, and I was the one who had decided to be "responsible" Priya. Instead, I could choose to do the really responsible thing: what was right for me.

Everything Happens for a Reason

After I moved back to London, I became involved in a relationship that wasn't good for either of us, and after a destructive few years, it came to an end. Once again I was devastated. Yet again, I had relegated my dreams, hopes, and desires to those of someone else and was not giving myself permission to do what I wanted. I had found myself giving away my freedom and all the responsibility for my life. As I healed from that relationship, I was also able to heal as I needed to from my marriage. In addition, I grew out of the many years of making myself subordinate to almost everyone else. My experience has been that when someone hasn't really worked on something, another event or someone else comes along to force the issue. Hopefully, the person eventually learns their lesson, and the experience and subsequent healing process is a metamorphosis.

Where I Landed

I now know that my opinion matters, and I feel worthwhile. I have good self-esteem and am confident in the things I know how to do. I know that I am the only one responsible for how I think, feel, and act. I am responsible for how good a daughter I am, how good a partner I am, how good a friend I am, how good a coach I am, and how good a colleague I am as well as how successful I am and for just about everything I allow to happen to me.

I know that the buck stops with me. I may fall short, but by experiencing a failure once in a while, I learn something, and in so doing, I increase my chances of success the following time. This understanding has given me an incredible sense of freedom to chart my own course in life. Freedom to listen to others without getting defensive or feeling attacked. Freedom to think I am good enough to be in this world and to interact with others. I also now I have the strength, ability, and freedom to make hard choices for myself. It is also easier to live with any fallout because I know I made the best decisions I could at the time given the information I had, and I respect myself for it, good or bad!

There are still loads of things I want to do and experience in life, but I am now free to give myself permission to figure out what they are and to pursue them. Hence, here I am, finally writing the book I always thought I would, because I want to help you get to a place of freedom too. It's not been easy, but I know I will never forgive myself if I don't forge ahead with dignity, tenacity, and resilience.

CHAPTER FIVE

Give YourSelf Permission to Know You Matter

⸻ ⁓⦾⧼⊙⧽⦿⁓ ⸻

When we create harmony in our minds and hearts, we will
find it in our lives. The inner creates the outer. Always.
—Louise L. Hay

⸻ ⁓⦾⧼⊙⧽⦿⁓ ⸻

Jack: A Story of Taking Care of Yourself

Earlier, we met my client, Jack. He had a lot of difficulty
caring for himself. He devoted himself to work, allowed
himself very little space to do what he wanted, and was really
quite unhappy. Together, we figured out that he was not devoting
enough time to doing the little things that made him feel good
about himself.

"But I never have any time for anything," Jack said. "When on
earth am I going to have time for a hobby? I barely have time
to just relax for ten minutes in the evening before going to bed."

I asked Jack to think about things that he had done in the past that made him happy. He thought for a while and then came up with something.

"Well," Jack said, "I really used to love taking radios apart with my father and putting them back together again."

"Okay," I said. "Why don't you do that?"

"But it's kind of silly. I mean, it's really pointless."

"Could you do it just for fun?" I asked. "Just something to fill your soul a little? Do you have somewhere that would be suitable for doing the work?"

"Yes," he told me. "I have a little shed at the bottom of the garden. I could do it in there."

After our session Jack went home and cleared some space in his garden shed. He started off grabbing fifteen minutes here and there, taking radios apart and putting them back together in working order. Maybe his family thought that his hobby was crazy, but it really didn't matter because it was *his* thing, and it made him happy. Most days he managed to find some time for himself. Quite quickly, his sense of self-worth grew because by giving himself a little time, he was valuing himself. He was honouring his own needs and the importance of having fun. The message that he was giving himself was that he deserved to have some time for his own interests – that he and the things he cared about were of value.

For a long time, this particular man had felt stuck in a rut at work and had longed to do something new but didn't seem to know how. In the process of learning how to value himself and his interests, he became confident enough to apply for a job he found more interesting. Jack was called for an interview and was offered the position. I never heard from him again after that, which is always a good sign that someone's life is proceeding along the lines they want it to! As a personal coach, becoming obsolete to any particular client means I have done my job well.

The Evolution of Knowing You Matter

You yourself, as much as anybody in the entire
Universe, deserve your love and affection.
—Buddha

The above story shows the importance of listening to yourself, paying attention to your needs, and acting upon them. It demonstrates how a little self-care, no matter how small or seemingly insignificant, can go a long way in building self-worth, self-esteem and confidence. As soon as we understand and feel that we completely matter in life and to ourselves, and therefore to others, the closer we are to reaching our best life possible.

From here, we will explore ways you can grow into *knowing* you matter and recognising that this knowledge is an important component of your ability to create happiness around you.

First, let me present a simple flow chart to illustrate the concept of getting to a place where you truly *know* and believe you matter, where you can demonstrate that to yourself and ultimately to others. People will only treat you the way you want to be treated when you show them how. If you're not treating yourself well, that is what they'll see and will invariably mirror.

The *Knowing* You Matter Pathway

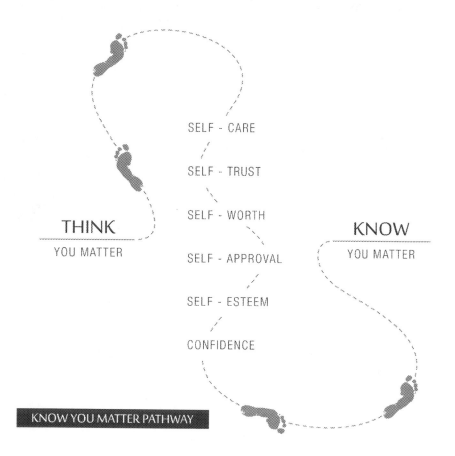

SELF - CARE

SELF - TRUST

SELF - WORTH

THINK

YOU MATTER

SELF - APPROVAL

KNOW

YOU MATTER

SELF - ESTEEM

CONFIDENCE

KNOW YOU MATTER PATHWAY

Figure 5:1: The Know You Matter Pathway

When it comes to your own life, giving yourself permission to do what you really want and need is absolutely essential. To let yourself do that, you need to learn how to come from a place of self-trust and self-worth.

You cannot live a happy, fulfilled life unless you trust, value, and respect yourself enough to truly take care of your needs. You build self-esteem by respecting your own physical, psychological, and spiritual needs, whatever they may be. I find that many people spend so much time worrying about what they need to do for others and what others think of them that they neglect to consider what they themselves need.

Think You Matter

The first step in the chart above is to *think* you matter. This can be a tall order if you don't really believe it, so at first, I urge you to suspend your disbelief and 'fake it 'till you make it'. It's all a mindset issue; start by forcing yourself to think you matter and that you are worthwhile.

Exercise: Putting Yourself First

Think of a few times when you put other people's needs before your own or have not done what was in your best interest because you thought something or someone else mattered more than you. Now identify what would have been in your best interest and why. Last, assess whether your actions have truly hurt anyone. For instance: Your friend likes this guy and has dragged you to five events this month alone to see him. He has no interest in her, and you're starting to get embarrassed, but you want to support your friend and you want her to like you. Now she wants you to go to another party. It's coming up to finals time and you have exams in some of your most difficult subjects. You really should study because you really need to get top grades so you can keep your scholarship. Your usual self, the one that's telling you that you don't matter as much as she does, would go to the party. If you did, you would essentially be saying to yourself and others and that you felt your friend's needs were more important more than yours. This is where the cycle of disrespecting yourself starts, and in doing so, you're also giving others permission to disrespect you. In reality, your friend has other people to go with (and even if she doesn't, that's not your responsibility), and she's actually just bullying you. It's up to you to be responsible for how your life turns out, and that exam could be a huge part of that! So, make an inventory of when you put others' needs first when you probably should have prioritised your own.

With just a little insight into when you're putting others' worth relative to your own and with some idea about when you can better support yourself, you'll be able to think and, hopefully, recognise that you matter. You are going to have to make a conscious effort at first. Some frustrations may surface as you realise when you've been giving your personal power away, but hold hard and don't get upset, as it's just not worth it.

Self-Care

I've often noticed that when people begin to truly take care of themselves, they start to look different. They've learned how to be more accepting of themselves and less concerned about presenting the incongruous or inauthentic appearance that they suppose the world expects of them. The process lifts a great amount of stress, and their physical bodies reflect the relief.

Most of all, learning to take care of yourself is about giving yourself permission to do things for yourself that nourish the soul. This can start with the basics, such as making sure that you eat properly, sleep well, and exercise enough.

I remember a client who absolutely loved to have fresh flowers in her home but who rarely bought them.

"I simply can't justify it," she said. "They're such an extravagance. I should be using that money for something more practical."

At the root of this woman's reluctance to do one simple, relatively inexpensive thing that made her life that little bit happier and more fulfilling was the fact that she wasn't giving herself permission to nurture herself the way she always tried to nurture other people.

We talked about her need to be kind to herself, and, tentatively at first, she began spending a little every week on fresh flowers. It was a small step, but the act of going to the florist, taking out the money, and buying a bunch of beautiful flowers was a big step towards learning how to value herself enough to do what would make her happy – what she needed – because she was worth it. That simple gesture made a big difference to her life. She now comes home to a fragrant house, made more beautiful by the blossoms and she knows she's done something in support of her own happiness. In so doing, she has communicated to herself that such ends were worthwhile.

Self-Trust

When you believe in or trust people, whether they are teachers, politicians, or any important individuals in your life, you respect them and, as a result, often follow their lead. You see these individuals as having high authority. I would suggest that you learn to place as much trust in yourself as you place in others so you recognise your own authority first and foremost.

We're going to go into more detail about trusting ourselves, others, and our gut instincts in "Chapter Eight: Give YourSelf Permission to be Brave". For now though, I will say that until you can trust what your instinct or subconscious is telling you, it will be difficult to confidently make the solid choices you need to make to live the life you want. In addition, if you don't practise trusting yourself, then you run the risk of either never truly trusting others or trusting those you shouldn't because you're unable to heed the warning signs your gut instinct may give you.

Self-Worth

Self-worth is what you get when you realise you matter and are worth taking care of. It comes once you start trusting yourself, and it will allow you to approve of yourself.

Self-Approval

When we don't consider ourselves worthwhile, we tend to seek approval from others. The problem with that is they approved of us in accordance with their agendas, values, or pre-conceptions. Our only hope is to move beyond seeking approval from others for the decisions we make and to learn how to give ourselves approval, because only we truly know what is in our best interest. Sure, we can ask for advice, but we shouldn't need to ask for approval.

By learning how to approve of your life and priorities, you nourish a sense of self-esteem that leads to living, thriving, and developing in a healthier environment. This also allows you to grow as an individual as well as a supportive and functioning member of your family and community.

Self-Esteem and Confidence

Although the terms *self-esteem* and *confidence* are often used interchangeably, they don't mean exactly the same thing but are, however, interrelated. *Self-esteem* in psychology means a person's overall evaluation or appraisal of their own worth. *Confidence* refers to that person's belief in themselves and their abilities. A person with high self-esteem cares for, loves, and respects themselves. They treat themselves well and expect others to do likewise. A confident person trusts their skills and what these demonstrate to the outside world. They believe that everything is going to be all right, as they have the ability to do what it takes to make it so.

Having good self-esteem is not simply a matter of feeling and appearing to be confident but of truly feeling that you're worthwhile and that you matter. You can be confident in your ability to do things without having self-esteem; however, when you grow a sense of self-worth, of true self-esteem, your confidence grows immensely. Conversely, a lack of self-esteem generally springs from a tendency to see others as more important than yourself.

I believe that real confidence grows from healthy self-esteem. This means that confidence comes from within and that you have control over it. True confidence is not arrogance, cockiness, or bravado. This sort of behaviour is a fake exterior that tends to push others away. True confidence is attractive.

Sometimes people confuse demonstrating self-esteem with self-centredness. They think that by considering themselves worthwhile, they devalue others. In my experience, the people who worry most about being selfish and self-absorbed are precisely the opposite. They worry about it so much that they often neglect to care for themselves and, without having to probe too far below the surface, it is evident that they have debilitating low self-esteem.

Know You Matter

By the end of this chapter, I hope you'll be closer to wholeheartedly, truly *believing* that you matter. When this happens you will start to understand that your needs, thoughts, desires, hopes, and contributions to your life and the lives of those around you are worthwhile and should be honoured. The first person you need to convince is yourself, and in time, this knowledge will become inherent and your self-care actions will become second nature.

Feeling like a Fraud

I've had clients who are hugely successful in their professional and personal lives but who struggle every day with the worry that they'll somehow be exposed as a fraud, despite the fact that all the evidence shows that they have earned all the respect they receive. They are still reacting to the messages they received during their childhoods. They have been told explicitly or have implicitly picked up the message that they are not good at something. Regardless of what happens, they always hear a little voice in their heads telling them that they are not good enough. They haven't yet learned how to give themselves permission to respect their own achievements. Until that time, they'll feel as though they don't deserve the acknowledgement or praise they receive from others. They focus on the incongruence between what they've been told or what they've perceived about themselves in the past and what they have actually achieved. This disconnect is where the fear of being a fraud lies, and one day, they worry, somebody will find out.

If you also feel this way, the goal is to close that gap. The best way to do that is to recognise that what was said is the past is either invalid or possibly inaccurate and then to focus on what you know to be true – in other words, to recognise what you've accomplished, achieved, qualified for, succeeded in, and so on. This concept will be addressed further in "Chapter Eight: Give YourSelf Permission to be Brave".

Defensiveness Rearing Its Ugly Head

I have frequently observed that people who don't value themselves find it difficult to care for themselves as well as they might need to and also tend to react defensively in their interactions with others. By believing in ourselves, we become better able to react proportionately to the things that happen and to what we're told.

Let's say, for instance, that a person goes out one day without realising that her hair is messy. Maybe her spouse or friend says, "Hey, look; your hair is all sticking up!"

If she doesn't value or care for herself, or even trust herself properly, she's liable to become defensive straight away in the face of what she interprets as a criticism. She'll assume that her spouse or friend is trying to hurt her feelings or is making fun of her appearance or is trying to undermine her confidence on a day when she needs to feel that things are going well. She might bristle and snap, "Can't you ever say anything nice to me?" or "What on earth is your problem? You know I have a big presentation today and need to feel relaxed!" She's been told that her hair is standing up, but the message she heard and took on board is "You're not good enough," when what she should have heard was probably along the lines of "I know you have a big presentation today, and I think it'll go better if you brush your hair first."

What was the real message? It was "Your hair is sticking up"; no more and no less. In fact, that is quite a useful piece of information, and it only takes a minute to find a comb or hairbrush and sort it out. But because this person's self-esteem, self-trust, and confidence are low, she perceived what was probably a piece of friendly advice as an attack and reacted strongly, in a way that was completely disproportionate to the situation. She got upset and angry about something that a more secure person would probably have forgotten about a few minutes after saying thanks and attending to the minor dilemma.

Exercise: Every Day, Do One Small Thing that Makes You Feel Fulfilled

I believe that we all deserve to do something for ourselves once in a while. Why not practise doing one small thing that makes you feel cared for every day? It doesn't have to be big – you can just treat yourself to an episode of that silly sitcom you enjoy or prepare *your* favourite dinner rather than someone else's. Or you can take fifteen minutes to sit in a quiet room or walk around the block and just relax. The world is not going to end just because you've given yourself permission to take a little time out.

Earlier, I talked about how making our needs primary is like putting on an oxygen mask in a stricken plane before attending to those who can't put on their masks by themselves. By caring for ourselves and attending to our own needs, we build trust in ourselves, and we become stronger. New opportunities open up for us, and we're able to venture into the world more boldly.

Caring for ourselves can start with something as simple as understanding what little things make us happy and nourish our sense of well-being, and then squeezing some time and space into the day for them.

Our Bodies as a Barometer for Our Lives

'Tis in ourselves that we are thus or thus. Our bodies are our gardens to which our wills are gardeners. —William Shakespeare, *Othello*

Whilst I know many factors can lead to illness, over the years since that original MS diagnosis, I've given a lot of thought to how our emotional and physical selves interact, and I've begun to see how closely they're linked.

On top of the immediate problem of the illness, I was still far from dealing with the underlying emotional problems that I had carried with me from childhood. I had run myself into the ground making sure I was doing everything I thought everybody else would think was right or proper. I didn't have enough confidence in myself that I could make the right decisions. Above all, I didn't listen to the messages that my body and mind were telling me loud and clear.

Now, I'm not saying that I wouldn't have developed MS if I had dealt with my emotional issues earlier and more effectively (although I do wonder, and there is a school of thought that believes that we manifest illness in our bodies when we have unresolved emotional issues[3]). However, my body, by way of fatigue, constant colds, and other little health oddities had been trying to tell me that something was wrong for years, and for years, I had ignored it.

Many people find that they are similarly discounting themselves, their personal needs, and their emotions. I believe that our bodies are accurate barometers, and if we listen to them and trust our gut instincts, they'll let us know when we're going down the wrong path. When we become ill, it's useful to explore our psychological well-being in addition to treating our physical ailments. I believe that we can mitigate the effects of illness, and even prevent illness from occurring in the first place, by being aware of our personal needs and emotions and how we can wholly support these aspects of our lives.

Celebrate Your Achievements

People just don't take the time to stop and acknowledge what they have achieved. It could be a very small accomplishment or a huge deal, but if we don't stop and take stock of it, we're essentially telling ourselves that what we've done doesn't matter, that it's not worthy

---

[3]   Christiane Northrop, MD, *Women's Bodies Women's Wisdom*, rev. ed., Piatkus (9 April 2009).

of acknowledgement or celebration. Now, I'm not talking balloons and cake (well, not always) but some sort of private or personal acknowledgement. Some people buy themselves a little trinket or that fancy vacuum they've been coveting. Others get a massage or have that very special glass of Champagne with friends or co-workers. The focus here is to take the time to praise yourself. When the mind and body get that positive reinforcement, they'll like it and will want more. You'll find it will become easier to do whatever it is you've set your mind to because you're kind to yourself when you reach your goals or achievements.

Know You Matter

This chapter was all about your getting to the point of truly believing that you matter just as much as everyone else, if not more. We discussed the tenets of how to achieve this by generally taking care of yourself and how feeling like a fraud and getting defensive will only put barriers in your way. Next it's time to have some fun, as by giving yourself permission to celebrate your achievements, you tell yourself you're worth it.

The Permission Journey: Stage 1

You've taken the first important steps of your journey, and having travelled from your home, you've now arrived in the Hawaiian Islands in the North Pacific Ocean. You've *given yourself permission to know you matter*, which is where you learned about your self-worth. The journey itself is the process – everything you have become aware of, everything you have learned, and everything you have started to implement in your everyday life.

Here are the questions I'll ask at the end of each chapter so you can gauge where you are and what you've learned. It's always good to take stock of how far you've come, and your answers to these questions will act as a celebration of sorts. Remember, it's all about taking souvenirs with you and leaving behind items that just weigh down your suitcase.

1) What did you learn for and about yourself in this chapter?
2) What tools or realisations are you going to take with you on your journey?
3) What traits, behaviours, thoughts, or memories are you going to leave behind?

Armed with your newfound self-worth, you're now able to embark on the next stage of your journey.

CHAPTER SIX

Give YourSelf Permission to Know What You Care About

Happiness is the state of consciousness which proceeds from the achievement of one's values
—*Ayn Rand*

It is really important to know which qualities you care about in life, and it's also very helpful to know which of them you want to live your life in accordance with. This can sound complicated at first, but when you get it, you'll find it's quite simple and immensely freeing. These qualities are often referred to as *values*.

What exactly is a value? The word is generally understood to mean the qualities of life you find important to maintain both your emotional and your physical well-being.

Life coaching puts great emphasis on knowing values. When I first started training as a coach, my mentor coach sent me a round of paperwork to fill out asking me what my values were. The problem with this was that I didn't really know what a value was. He then explained that a value is a trait that I know to be important in the functioning of my everyday life. Wow! At the time, that could have meant anything for me, so for a few years, I muddled along using this concept whilst not really knowing how to embody it.

Then one day I worked with a fabulous strategist, my friend and mentor Deri ap John Llewellyn Davies. He constantly harped on about values, and I sheepishly went along with him. Rather stridently, I pretended that I knew what he was talking about. We were working on whether I was going to go into partnership with a very prestigious coach and her organisation. It looked like a great idea, but something was wrong, and my gut instinct was troubling me. Deri asked me what about the coach and the organisation was bothering me.

"I have problems with the way they're communicating with me," I told him.

"Well," Deri said, "that's what you hold valuable: communication! If they're not working within one of your core values, you're always going to feel out of sorts or uncomfortable. Now you get to choose whether it's worth powering through because there's something to gain in the long run."

When I examined the situation, I felt that the organisation had a "less-is-more" approach to communication, and I knew that I couldn't work like that. If there is a lack of communication between me and anyone I work with (or, indeed, interact with in anyway) I find I don't trust the situation or the person, my understanding of what is going on is weakened and my security within it is threatened. If my core value of communication isn't met, I'm unlikely to feel comfortable, and in turn, I'll not be at my best.

At that point, the concept of values and their role in my life became very clear to me.

Core Values

In this context, values are more essential to us than our personal or physical needs (although these are important as well) as our values guide what we feel we need from life.

When we find ourselves feeling ill at ease, this is often because we're living in a way that is out of sync with our core values. Only we have the ability and right to construct a life for ourselves that is in accordance with what we believe to be appropriate and healthy for us.

People setting up a business are generally advised to come up with a brief mission statement that succinctly sums up what they want to achieve and what their business's core values are. Google's famous value statement is "Don't be evil". Individuals can come up with personal mission statements too, ones that guide their actions and communicate their desires. Mine might be something like, "Be a catalyst of change." What would yours be?

At the root of all personal or business mission statements are values, which can be accessible or tangible concepts such as family, work, or respect. More often than not, however, they are emotions like love, peace, and grace or behavioural traits and characteristics like communication, nobility, and honour.

When you start getting to grips with your values, you'll more than likely find that they're a mixed bag. Still, it's good to have a list you can call your own that you can work with as you apply it to your everyday life. Values can also be fun, mystical, obscure or frivolous – they don't have to be grand and highfalutin! I remember feeling guilty and full of shame when I started to see that beauty, luxury, and comfort were important to me. I thought that these were all rather shallow and that one needed to be rich to have such things. Then I realised that beauty need not be equated with a high price tag – beautiful objects and surroundings can be found on any budget; they may not cost any more than opening your eyes and seeing the good around you.

Something to keep in mind is that as we grow, our values change. Our fundamental values tend to remain static, but sometimes as we gain wisdom and information, they evolve and adapt. It's also often difficult to come up with an initial values list, so here's a little help.

Exercise: Know Your Values

I work quite intensively with my clients on values, and they often find this work the most challenging. Knowing your values is the foundation to understanding yourself; not knowing them can get in the way of really giving yourself permission to think big. Usually, I don't like giving people a list to choose from for fear of implanting ideas; however, identifying one's values can sometimes be rather difficult, so in this situation, I feel that a list may have some benefit, and I've included one here. Of course, this list is by no means comprehensive; it's intended only as a place to start. Sometimes it's easier to recognise a value than to dig around and come up with one. In time, however, you will start seeing patterns in your behaviour, traits, likes and dislikes, and you'll be able to come up with a list all of your own.

You may notice that integrity isn't on the list. That's because I believe that when we live in accordance with our values, *then* we live with integrity.

For now, here's a list of potential values to get you started. Pick or come up with five to start a short list of your own:

Communication   Beauty   Serenity

Authenticity   Respect   Organisation

Harmony   Tenacity

Teamwork   Connection   Peace

Collaboration   Autonomy   Abundance

Nobility   Fun   Love

Honesty   Commitment   Creativity

Spontaneity   Dignity   Positivity

Compassion   Loyalty

Synergy   Adventure   Grace

Spirituality   Charm   Learning

Curiosity

Supportive   Money

Empathy   Security   Family

Solitude

Purpose   Success   Meaning

Supremacy   Trust   Awareness

Faith   Freedom

Figure 6:1: Values

Values as a Road Map

So, as you've seen, your values are traits and characteristics by which you live. They can also serve as a road map for your life. Knowing your values can give you permission to make the right decisions for yourself. By interacting with this list, you'll always have something to guide you.

As in my recent example, I understood the benefit of knowing my values when I needed to make a decision or a structured plan. As a coach, I work within this framework with my clients. It is really important for them to identify their values at the outset, before they try to make any other choices. So, have a go at the exercise below and see how it works for you. If at first you have trouble, keep the exercise in your mind and come back to it when you have finished this chapter.

Exercise: Reading the Road Map

1) Write the question or issue you are struggling to make a decision about on a blank piece of paper.
2) Write a list of your top five values on a small card that you can keep with you at all times.
3) With your values list in one hand and the question in the other, ask yourself if the issue you are deliberating on is aligned with your values.

For instance, suppose the issue is: "Should I take the new job I've been offered?"

Your list of values might include autonomy, communication, learning, and abundance. This job pays quite well, so abundance is covered. You know that you'll be micro-managed because the person who interviewed you, who will be your manager, was very regimented, nit-picky, and particular about the format of your résumé. His communication style was abrasive and defensive. Your values of autonomy and communication may not be fulfilled, and therefore, maybe the job isn't right for you.

However, another value of yours is learning, and you very much want to break into this new industry. The job offer ticks the boxes for learning and abundance, but not autonomy and communication. At this juncture, you can make a choice. Which values matter most to you? Which do you need to survive in one piece? Are there any you can live without so you can reap the rewards? If making more money so that you can pay off your college loans quicker and breaking into a new industry are most important to you and you can live with being managed intensively and spoken to strongly, then take the job. In this instance, you know what you're getting into, and you will have to take personal responsibility and anticipate how to communicate with your new boss. However, if you simply cannot live with being spoken to unpleasantly and micro-managed, you cannot take the job, regardless of how useful the experience will be and how much money you'll make. The choice is all yours.

By inherently knowing your specific values you can have more faith in your decisions and be better able to stand by them. At the same time, you'll know what you're getting into and may need to adjust to in certain situations.

Values in Relationships

Whenever I meet a new client, a red flag goes up if they state that one of their values is to be loved and respected by others. That means that their happiness, well-being, and very existence depend on other people's behaviour, or on getting others to do what the client "needs"

71

them to do. Good luck with that! I know from my own experience that this doesn't work. Trying to make others do what I want them to do has only ever left me depleted and frustrated.

When people love, respect, praise, or support you, this is a by-product of *your* behaviour. It is what happens when people see you and want to be around you. It is what you get in return for taking personal responsibility. Like leadership, it's earned, not commanded.

In any relationship, intimate or otherwise, there can be a moment when it becomes clear that the other person's value system is not the same as your own. This doesn't mean that one system is worse than the other; simply that you do not prioritise the same things. Over the years, I've learned that for me, it's very important to know what others' values are and how they stand in relation to mine. Particularly in the context of close friendships, there has to be a reasonable amount of synchronicity. The things that I care about, that make up my core values, include open communication, respect, diligence, and comfort and beauty. In important relationships, it really matters to me that people can communicate well and don't play games. If someone would rather watch a football match than go out with me one particular evening, that is okay – but making up an excuse or lying is not.

Since we all grew up in unique families, each of which with its own mini-culture, and because we're all members of a broader society, it can sometimes be hard to figure out which values are truly our own and which are really the property of the people around us or of society at large. If we have simply borrowed them and they're on loan, we can give them back. You might borrow a friend's jumper because it looks great on her only to realise that it does nothing for you at all. The same applies to values. You can acknowledge and respect someone else's values without feeling that you need to prioritise exactly the same things in the same way.

When I was at university in the UK, I lived in a flat without heating above a dry cleaner's. It was so damp that I often woke to find my hair plastered to the pillowcase and the essay I had written the night before wrinkled from humidity. When I moved in, all my room contained was a small bed, a grimy built-in desk, a wardrobe, and a single light bulb hanging from the ceiling – depressing! Although money had been scarce the majority of my teenage years, my mother always made a point of keeping our house pretty, so this was what I was used to. Faced with this dreary space, I knew I had to do something, as I wouldn't be happy living without a little cheeriness in my surroundings. I had virtually no money at this point, but I had taken out a credit card, so I decided some home furnishings were in order. I found and purchased a blue-and-white frilly lampshade for the hanging light bulb, a matching cushion, and a complementing stuffed toy dog to go on my bed. I valued these three items dearly. They provided comfort, elegance, and beauty and made me feel safe in a very cold, scary, smelly, and lonely room. These values were important to me, but it soon became clear my flatmates did not share them. When they saw what I had bought they told everyone else, who bullied and teased me for being posh and a rich bitch. It was hard for me, and in addition to a multitude of other reasons, it led to my leaving the university. If, at the time, I had only understood that I was living authentically and in accordance with my own values I would have been able to understand that it did not matter what my flatmates thought. I could have either engaged with them, as they were absolutely living in accordance with their values, or I could have turned away. Either way I could have given myself permission to stand behind what mattered to me and life would have been much easier.

Nobody grows up in a vacuum; we are all deeply influenced by the cultures in which we develop and learn, and by the people in our immediate circles. Nonetheless, there can be huge differences between people – even members of the same family! Accepting that we have our own values and that we are all entitled to an opinion and the right to live as we see fit can be difficult.

Why We Need to Value Ourselves

Regardless of what is going on in our lives, ultimately we are the only ones who can decide how we live. Of course, we'll always have responsibilities and chores to attend to, whether at work or at home, but we can choose to get ourselves to a space where these are what we *want* to do. As we'll see in "Chapter Nine: Give YourSelf Permission to be Happy", even when a job is only necessary to pay the bills, we can learn to focus on the aspects that we find fulfilling and let go emotionally of the conditions that bring us down.

People will always feel that doing things explicitly for themselves is selfish, that the only things worth doing are those that make life better for others. I would argue that taking care of ourselves makes us much better equipped to also care for the people in our lives. Certainly, it's important for everyone to use their talents, gifts, and strengths for the good of others as well as themselves, but by giving ourselves permission to quietly value and care for ourselves first, then we can be there for others in an empowering rather than a draining way.

If you want to get involved in volunteering, for example, do so by all means, but get involved with an activity that you enjoy. If you love to garden, you could look into local schemes to help people with their allotments. If you love sports and physical activity, you could look into sharing that passion in a way that will be enriching to others as well as yourself by running after-school physical education programs or helping the disabled or elderly with their mobility.

Many people spend their lives running around trying to do their best for and to impress others. The great irony is that we do our best for others when we engage with them in a way that is fulfilling and meaningful for us as well. Helping to make the world a better place doesn't have to be about sacrifice; it can be about enrichment, fun, and opportunity. It can be about valuing our true selves and our real strengths and abilities so that we share them with others.

Deciding to honour yourself and your values, and acting upon this decision, gives you the freedom to give yourself permission to do what it takes to make sure that those values are met.

Other Ways to Explore Your Values

As you may have seen, it can be very difficult to figure out what your values are. As you've been working on self-worth, taking care of yourself, and listening to yourself, let's now try another way to identify your values.

You can work on this alone, but you might find it more productive to brainstorm with a coach, therapist, trusted friend, close family member, business mentor, or a religious or spiritual leader.

Exercise: Which Films Inspire You Most?

A private way to start exploring what your values are is by listing a few films that have inspired you over the years. Once you've identified the films, make a list of the qualities that you relate to in each film.

If films aren't your thing, you can carry out the exercise with TV shows, books, songs, or whatever touches you the most.

For instance, here is my honest list:
Monsoon Wedding: heritage, respect, beauty, honour

Platoon: honour, nobility, tenacity
Alice in Wonderland: free abandon, freedom
The Blind Side: resilience, persistence, love, family
Cars: friendship, loyalty, fun
Schindler's List: respect, compassion, vision
Argo: triumph, honour, creativity
Rocky Horror Picture Show: fun, edginess, kitsch
Lawrence of Arabia: maverick, grandeur, spectacle

Now take a look at your list of films and qualities. Do any of them resonate with you? Could they be your values? Pick and choose from them wisely and carefully, but also be honest and stretch yourself.

Know Your Values

When you know and understand your values, you gain insight into yourself. Most importantly, you have a road map that will help you make decisions. You can use your newfound understanding to gain deeper insight into why you feel the way you do in any given situation. You can honour those feelings and work hard to make sure that you act and live in a way that is consistent with your values and that your values, and, by extension, *you*, are worth as much care and consideration as anyone else.

The Permission Journey: Stage 2

So here we are at your second stop in the Society Islands in the South Pacific Ocean having travelled the journey of giving yourself permission to know what you care about. During this time, you've recognised and engaged with your values. The journey itself is the process – everything you have become aware of, everything you have learned, and everything you have started to implement in your everyday life.

Here are the same questions you saw at the end of the last chapter, but this time, hold your values in the forefront of your mind as you answer them. As before, these questions allow you to gauge where you are and what you've learned. As always, it's good to take stock of how far you've come, and your answers to these questions will act as a celebration of sorts. Remember, it's all about taking souvenirs with you and leaving behind items that just weigh down your suitcase.

1) What did you learn for and about yourself in this chapter?
2) What tools or realisations are you going to take with you on your journey?
3) What traits, behaviours, thoughts, or memories are you going to leave behind?

Armed with your newfound values, you're now able to embark on the next stage of your journey.

CHAPTER SEVEN

Give YourSelf Permission to Take Back Your Life

Each player must accept the cards life deals him or her:
but once they are in hand, he or she alone must decide
how to play the cards in order to win the game.
—Voltaire

Your Best PR

The only way to take back your life is to take personal responsibility for it. That means taking ownership of everything you do, think, and feel.

When you were a child, your parents or guardians were responsible for your life and for all your needs. As you grew up, you gradually took over responsibility for more and more as you learned how to go to bed by yourself, how to brush your teeth, how to do your homework, and so on. We have all been through much the same process.

In the context of growing up, most of us have learned how to take responsibility for our own daily needs, but taking personal responsibility for our own choices, happiness, and well-being can be more difficult. At times, for one reason or another, the transfer of these responsibilities from parent to child doesn't happen the way it should. Often after a trauma like divorce, a death in the family, or illness, a parent may be unwilling or unable to allow their child to make their own decisions. This is commonly known as not being able to let go. Equally, the child may be afraid of moving away from the security of their parents.

As a coach, one of the things I hear most often is that people feel that they simply cannot live the life they've always wanted because they have other responsibilities and duties, such as spouses and children, elderly parents, or demanding jobs. Personally, I was convinced that there were many things that I would never be able to do because my mother wouldn't approve or because they weren't appropriate for a girl from my socio-economic background.

Seema: A Story of Learning How to Take Personal Responsibility

I worked with one client who was an extremely bright young woman of seventeen who seemed to be almost paralysed by her mother's success.

Seema's mother was a high-achieving businesswoman who had worked extremely hard all her life. She fled her homeland in eastern Europe with virtually nothing and had been able to build a very comfortable life for her and her daughter in the UK. However, her daughter had, inadvertently, picked up the message that there was no way she could measure up to her mother, so there was no point in even trying.

Seema claimed, quite calmly, that she was perfectly happy doing nothing in particular and hoped to marry a man who would keep her in designer shoes.

As we worked together, Seema was able to figure out that this apparent apathy sprang from a fear of never being as good as her mother, whom she admired so much. That understanding started to set her free, and she became able to try challenges that she had never taken on before – challenges different to those her mother had confronted. She started the process of becoming her own person. She also started measuring herself by her own success in attaining her goals and aspirations rather than by someone else's measure.

We were able to reach the stage at which she recognised that she did aspire to more than marriage to a wealthy man. As her sense of personal responsibility grew, I could see a real shift in the way she presented herself. Her clothing style changed, she started to take greater care with her hair and makeup, and she stood up straight as she walked.

One day, she came in and said that she had been talking to a friend about Ramadan[4]. "My family's never been very religious at all," she said, "so we don't observe the fast. But I'd really like to see if I could do it. I don't want to change my lifestyle or anything, but I'd like to understand my roots and take on the challenge of fasting."

This was the first time I had heard her saying anything so proactive, and I realised that it would be a huge accomplishment for her. That year she fasted for thirty days, which was difficult

---

[4] Ramadan is the ninth month of the Muslim calendar where fasting takes place during daylight hours.

because nobody else in her immediate family was doing it, although her grandparents and some uncles and aunts supported her. When the fasting period was over, Seema experienced a wonderful feeling of achievement. For the first time ever, she knew what it was like to take responsibility for herself. In response, her mother, whose personal drive and ambition had made her so successful, learned how to step back in order to trust her daughter to make her own decisions and take responsibility for them. They became closer as a result. And, now that she knew that she was capable of real achievement, Seema started to think about attending university. Something she had never contemplated before. Having given herself permission to take on that one challenge, she had learned how to give herself permission to try more and that she didn't always have to compare herself to her mother or anyone else.

Control

In the long run, we shape our lives, and we shape ourselves. The process never ends until we die. And the choices we make are ultimately our own responsibility.
—Eleanor Roosevelt

The first step in taking back your life is to realise and understand exactly what you have control over and what you are responsible for. Understanding what we can control and what we cannot is truly liberating. For example, none of us can change the family or circumstance into which we were born. We can't change the past or undo decisions we've made prior to the present moment. What we can do is control how we react to each situation and take positive steps to create a future that is incrementally closer to how we want to live.

Way too many people go through life agonising over things that they have no control over. People think, "If only Dad hadn't drunk so much," or "If only my colleagues were different; if only they understood me better," or "If only so-and-so would change; I would be so much happier." Even victims of assault and rape often say, "If only I hadn't decided to walk home on my own," or "If I had just taken a taxi instead." Whilst I understand why people feel this way, it pains me to see them thinking along these lines. These beliefs will only arrest their healing and keep their lives stagnant.

Understanding that there are things we simply cannot control, regardless of how hard we try, frees us to live in the present and plan for the future. As much as we'd like to, we cannot change past events. We can support the people in our lives, but we cannot change their fundamental ways of being and thinking.

Sometimes, though, we can influence certain situations by our own actions. Whilst we cannot make someone like us or do business with us, we can influence the situation by taking control of what we can, such as our behaviour and our actions. The key to influencing a situation is to do as much groundwork as possible then let go and allow the other party to come to the table when the time is right for them. Once we recognise where we can influence a situation, we free ourselves up to live immensely powerful lives.

How to Identify What You Can Control

———⟊⟊⟊⟊⟊———

Worry pretends to be necessary but
serves no useful purpose.
—Eckhart Tolle

———⟊⟊⟊⟊⟊———

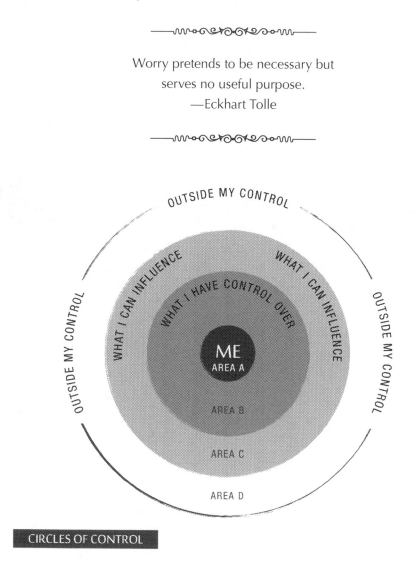

Figure 7:1: Circles of Control

When I work with people as a coach, we explore various scenarios in their lives, looking at them from all angles. On some level, they've always known that they have no control over many of the things they worry about and should let go of them to free up their energy for the things they do have control over or can influence. Recognising and accepting this is very important. The Circles of Control,[5] although seemingly simple, strikes a resounding chord with many people.

There are many things we cannot control, for example, the weather, an overbearing boss's tirade, or a judgemental friend's criticism. We can, however, control how we react to them. We have control over how we communicate with others. In fact, the way we do this is how we influence others. For instance, you can encourage your employees to work the way you want them to by highlighting where they've done well in their jobs. Provide them with positive feedback that encourages their continued success, and you'll support them in doing tasks the way you want them to be done. In addition, try disseminate negative feedback in a positive, rather than accusatory, manner.

Ultimately, you need to give yourself permission to believe in yourself and take charge of your emotions and reactions to the things that happen to you whilst also accepting that what happens in other people's lives is their business.

You can use the following exercise in your everyday life and in specific situations to figure out what you can control and what you cannot. You can learn how to simply let go of what you have no control over and, in so doing, cease the anxiety and worry associated with it. Then, you can give yourself permission to focus your energy and attention on what you do have control over. Once you know what you have control over, it'll be easier to wield influence in the relevant areas. This is a quick way to free yourself from worry and to allow your brain more time to rest or think more constructively.

---

[5]   This is a tool with various versions used both in psychology and coaching. It comes under many different names, including Circle of Influence, Sphere of Control, and Sphere of Influence.

Exercise: Apply the Concept of the Circles of Control

Often, seeing the concept on paper brings a person's anxieties and issues to the forefront of their consciousness, which can be tremendously liberating.

So, to practise figuring out what you can control, what you can influence and what you cannot control, pick an issue you want to work on, something that's troubling you and that you want to reach a conclusion about.

Take a look at figure 7:1 and draw the three circles on a piece of paper. Write your name in the bullseye (Area A). Then, outside the third circle (Area D), write down what you do **not** have control over. Then, write down what you **do** have control over in the second circle (Area B). Once you've identified those elements, you can assess what you might have influence over, and write those down in the third circle (Area C).

I could implement the concept in the following way:

I live with a chronic illness, and, therefore, I live with a lot of uncertainty. I cannot change the fact that I have MS, and there is no point in agonising over whether things would be better if it had been diagnosed earlier or fantasising that if I had done things differently, I may not have developed the illness at all. I have **no control** over these issues.

I can **control** my attitude towards the condition. I can engage with my health-care providers in finding the treatments that work best for me. I can live a healthy lifestyle and take care of my mind and body so that I'm in the best possible condition. In so doing, I'm in a better position to **influence** the course and progression of the disease. Above all, I can choose not to let a situation that is not of my own making take over my life and destroy my happiness. I can take control of my mindset and my behaviour.

We all have things in our lives that we need to deal with. Understanding which areas we have control over and which we do not can really help us start to make changes towards obtaining the lives we want.

The Blame Game

—————ᴡᴡᴏ꙰ꙮꙮꙮꙮꙮᴡᴡ—————

Nobody can make you feel inferior
without your permission.
—Eleanor Roosevelt

—————ᴡᴡᴏ꙰ꙮꙮꙮꙮꙮᴡᴡ—————

Part of learning how to take responsibility for ourselves is acquiring the ability to step away from blaming. It's easy for anyone to fall into the trap of pointing a finger and saying, "But it's his fault! I can't have the life I want because he won't let me!"

Admittedly some people have experienced truly horrendous trauma, where it would be acceptable to blame the perpetrator. The media comments about how people's lives will never be the same again, that they will always be damaged and broken as a result of a dreadful event. The media are correct – victims' lives will never be the same again – but many have not allowed their lives to be broken forever. They have chosen, with incredible willpower, to have faith and trust in themselves, to not remain cast as a victim but to understand that what happened happened in the past and that the only option for self-preservation is to move forward.

Most of us have struggled with issues that are far less egregious but that still have a profound impact on our lives. Whilst we cannot change the past or control everything in our lives, we don't have to let those factors that are beyond our control take away our power.

I personally know how it can be easier to play the victim, to rely on the blame game, than to take responsibility. There were times when I hid behind the MS diagnosis more than was warranted at the time and I blamed my family members for relying on me too much and putting too much pressure on me.

On the flip side, some people feel silly for being upset or for struggling with issues that look far less serious than some of the dreadful events others have suffered. When a client tries to dismiss something that has happened to them or their feelings around it by saying, "Well, other people have been through much worse," I stop them for a moment and say, "But wait, it's all relative. You're allowed to acknowledge how you feel. You're allowed to say it hurt or that you were scared. What counts now is how you move on from here."

We need to look at what is really going on. Sure, some people have been very badly treated by others, and this treatment may well have been very damaging. Nobody is suggesting that everything needs to be forgiven and forgotten. But what we can do is learn to accept responsibility for the ways in which we continue to react to events after they occur. No matter how big or small the infraction or issue seems, we can refuse to be victimised twice. We can seize control of our own lives and emerge stronger from the experience.

Recognising this does not mean that you should feel bad about the challenges that sometimes drag you down. You can start to deal with them by giving yourself permission to recognise that they might be holding you back but can be overcome or moved past. You can work through those feelings towards a solution once you've identified the obstacles. You can start by giving yourself permission to grow strong and happy despite whatever has been holding you back. You don't have to dismiss or ignore feelings of hurt, pain, or anger because you think they're not important enough. You can accept them for what they are and choose to move on anyway. I meet people all the time who ultimately deal quite successfully with the fallout of truly difficult childhoods.

Moving Away from Guilt

Many people feel guilty about putting themselves first or saying no to other people. I remember once looking up the meaning of *guilt* with a client. What we discovered is that guilt is a perceived emotion, which is generally tied to a doing something horribly wrong on purpose. Pay particular attention to the italicised words, they reflect the harsh nature of the word guilt.

According to *Merriam-Webster's Dictionary*: Guilt:[6]

1: the fact of having committed a *breach* of conduct especially *violating* law and involving a penalty; broadly: guilty conduct

2 a: the state of one who has committed an offense *especially consciously*

b: feelings of culpability especially for *imagined* offenses or from a sense of inadequacy

Guilt is a strong emotion and can make one feel really awful, but is it always warranted? Consider these questions when those niggling feelings of guilt arise: Did you consciously go out of your way to do harm to someone? Did you do something terrible and very hurtful, or did you just not do something someone else wanted you to do? Was

---

6   http://www.merriam-webster.com/dictionary/guilt

what they wanted you to do reasonable, or did you feel like it was too much? Be honest with yourself.

Sometimes it's really difficult to give ourselves permission to say no to doing what others want us to do because we're afraid of feeling guilty. We would rather put our needs last than deal with the perceived guilt.

Guilt is often only that: perceived. We often think that others will be upset with us if we don't do what they want us to. Sometimes they *will* be upset, but often that's not our responsibility. Most times, we just assume that they will think badly of us when, in fact, they probably won't.

As difficult as an MS diagnosis seemed to me at first, I perversely realised that having a chronic illness had many advantages too. For as long as I could remember I devoted a huge amount of effort to taking care of others. I worked very hard to protect my mother and ran around doing things for her. I also felt incredibly guilty if I didn't spend every free moment with my grandmother. I had been so busy trying to be responsible for everyone else that I didn't even know what taking personal responsibility meant. So, whilst being diagnosed with MS was painful and difficult on many levels, it also was of benefit to me. I was able to use the fact that I was sick as an excuse to say no without feeling the guilt I had so often experienced before. I could say that I was tired, that I needed to take my medication, or that I needed to just focus on me and my needs without the stigma of appearing selfish. So, with the diagnosis, all of a sudden, I found a way to give myself permission to say no.

The problem was that it only worked as long as I held on to my disease. As soon as I started to get better and gain both emotional and physical strength, I wanted to start living a normal life, but I soon realised that I had a conflict. If I wanted to feel better and move past my diagnosis,

I had to shed its label and everything that went with it, including the ability to hide behind it and use it as an excuse, thus misguidedly eluding feelings of guilt. I had to overcome the fear of the disease and start taking personal responsibility for myself independently of anything else. I had experienced what it was like to feel free and to give myself permission to take care of myself first and say no to things without the guilt. I now had to give myself permission to make my own decisions because I thought they were the best choice for me. I needed to know that there would be a day when I was well, but I still wanted to live the guilt-free, honest, and responsible life that my diagnosis had made possible. Unfortunately, there are still days when I have to say no to something I would have loved to have done but cannot because of my health. I am now at a place where I use ramifications to my health as a reason to say no, not as an excuse. And I don't always like it, but it is the new reality. Ultimately, we still have to take care of ourselves otherwise we are no good to anyone in the long run.

However, sometimes, when it comes to *exercising* the muscle of giving yourself permission to live your life or even just saying no, you might want to come up with a harmless excuse, like "I have to work," "I need to wash my hair," or "I have to help a friend" – to try saying no on for size, as it were. Where do you have to lose the guilt?

Natasha: A Story of Charting One's Own Course

———∽∿∾∿∾———

Remember always that you not only have the right to
be an individual, you have an obligation to be one.
—Eleanor Roosevelt

———∽∿∾∿∾———

A lovely woman came to see me because she was very unhappy at work. "I'm sick of always following the same routine," she said, "and

I'm fed up with my boss. She is just so difficult and demanding, and it's really very difficult to feel enthusiastic and happy every morning when I head off to the office."

Natasha worked for one of the biggest advertising firms in the world and was in charge of one of the company's most important accounts. She had a good salary and most of the people she knew assumed that she was really enjoying her snazzy job and her great apartment. Little did they know about what was really going on.

"Occasionally there's a challenge at work that's fun," she said, "but mostly I just feel uninspired by what I do all day. I'm fed up. I need a change, but I don't know what I want to do."

As we worked together, it soon became apparent that what others thought about her and her career was vital to her. She felt that she needed to know that she was doing the right thing, and it was crucial that other people approved of her decisions and how she approached her life. This became quite tiring for her.

Natasha had grown up in a very strict household. Her father was domineering, and held very strong opinions on how she should behave, who she could and could not spend time with, how she should dress, and, in general, how she should represent the family. Unsurprisingly, her father also had very clear ideas of what were worthwhile career options for Natasha and what were not.

As we explored what Natasha found inspiring, we soon realised that she liked to be creative and that colour and flair were important to her. It turned out that she had long dreamed of starting an online fashion business. However, after much thought and planning, she decided against it.

"If you really want to work in fashion," I asked her one day, "why don't you?"

I already believed that Natasha had enough business experience coupled with a real passion for clothes to be hired by a reputable company. There didn't seem to be any good, objective reason for her not to pursue her dream.

After discussing the matter for a while, Natasha admitted that she had never seriously considered a job in fashion to be an option, as her father would not have seen it as a worthwhile focus for a career. By this stage, we had worked a lot on her need to take care of herself and to do things in line with what really mattered to her, and not just focusing on what others expected of her.

Acknowledging that she had been holding herself back because she was worried about what her father might think or do, Natasha was able to understand that she wanted to live according to her needs and wants. And what she wanted was to work in fashion, so she set the wheels in motion.

At our next session, Natasha excitedly told me that, out of the blue, a headhunter had approached her about a position in one of Britain's largest fashion houses. She was perfectly qualified for the job and was offered it a few days after the interview.

Amazing! Somewhere in the past, Natasha had decided that what she really cared about wasn't really important. Ultimately, it all boiled down to her father's issues and her need for him to feel pleased with her. Once she was able to clear the block and take back her life she was suddenly presented with a life-changing opportunity!

Sweeping Your Side of the Street

I often ask clients if they have "swept their side of the street". If we envision our lives as a row of houses, we can imagine how each occupant is only responsible for clearing autumn leaves or snow from the area in front of their own property. They might look disapprovingly at the mess in front of the house across the street, but its upkeep isn't really any of their business, and it certainly isn't their responsibility. We can always help our neighbours, but we cannot do their work for them. If the mess is in someone else's front yard, legally we're not even allowed to go onto their property without permission!

When issues arise in our lives, we need to ask ourselves if we've done whatever is most responsible in the given situation. Have we taken control over those elements that are within our circle of control? Have we done what we're supposed to do in a way that's consistent with what we believe to be important?

When we're able to take responsibility for our own lives and sweep our side of the street, life becomes more manageable. As we spend less time wrestling with the mess outside other people's houses, it becomes easier for us to be more authentic as our real selves and to be proud to invite others over for a barbecue in our yard.

Once I understood that I was making decisions for myself based on others' circumstances and desires, I started to look around and pay attention to what I would like to do. I decided I wanted to move back to London from Los Angeles. I wouldn't be a less responsible daughter and granddaughter if I no longer ran around trying to organise every aspect of other people's lives. In fact, I could be a better daughter and granddaughter by being responsible for myself. I could stop blaming my family situation for the things that I perceived as being wrong with my life, and I could love and support my family members from a position of trust. I could trust them to care for themselves and ask for help when they needed it. I would always be there for them. At the same time, I had to trust in myself to make the decisions that were right for me. It was such a relief to take personal responsibility, to sweep my side of the street and to leave others to maintain their own properties.

Francesca: A Story of Taking Back Her Life

When I worked with Francesca, she was struggling with alcoholism and, by extension, had never given herself permission to think about what she really wanted for her life. She gave most of her money away and spent the rest on wine and designer clothes she couldn't afford. She was distraught because she knew that her behaviour was having a big impact on her relationship with her young daughter. Having confirmed that she was dealing with her addiction by attending AA meetings and working with a sponsor, I worked with her on how she could manage her debt, how she could restructure her work so that she could spend more time with her child, and how she could finally give herself permission to take charge of her life. She had to make some painful decisions, including moving to a smaller house and selling her car, but she worked through them. Most importantly, as she became able to assume a leadership position in her own life, she stopped giving her money away, she took control of her drinking, she spent quality time with her daughter, and she ultimately was able to live more peacefully and authentically.

Take Back Your Life

—⁓ↄⱺⱹↄⱺↄↄⱺ⁓—

If you could kick the person in the pants responsible for
most of your trouble, you wouldn't sit for a month.
—Theodore Roosevelt

—⁓ↄⱺⱹↄⱺↄↄⱺ⁓—

Sometimes all that is necessary to start this journey is to realise that the
only obstacle to achieving the life you want is yourself. The first step to
combating your blockage is to grant yourself the permission and trust
to just get started.

It can be unnerving to give yourself permission to take personal
responsibility, and you may encounter many challenges along the way,
but in the end, doing so will free you to make the choices that will
enable you to create the life you've always wanted. Doesn't that make
it worth the effort? I think it does!

The Permission Journey: Stage 3

So here we are at your third stop in the Sandwich Islands, in the
South Atlantic Ocean. You have travelled the journey of giving
yourself permission to take back your life, which basically involves
taking personal responsibility for everything you think, feel, and do.
The journey itself is the process – everything you have become aware
of, everything you have learned, and everything you have started to
implement in your everyday life.

Here's the same set of questions you've seen in previous chapters, but
this time, hold your responsibilities in the forefront of your mind as you
answer them. As before, these questions allow you to gauge where you
are and what you've learned. As always, it's good to take stock of how

far you have come, and your answers to these questions will act as a celebration of sorts. Remember, it's all about taking souvenirs with you and leaving behind items that just weigh down your suitcase.

1) What did you learn for and about yourself in this chapter?
2) What tools or realisations are you going to take with you on your journey?
3) What traits, behaviours, thoughts, or memories are you going to leave behind?

Armed with your newfound sense of personal responsibility, you're now able to embark on the next stage of your journey.

Give YourSelf Permission to Be Brave

⎯⎯ ᴀᴠᴠᴏᴏᴄᴇᴛᴏᴏᴛᴇᴏᴏᴠᴠ ⎯⎯

I learned that courage was not the absence of fear,
but the triumph over it. The brave man is not he who
does not feel afraid, but he who conquers that fear.
—Nelson Mandela

⎯⎯ ᴀᴠᴠᴏᴏᴄᴇᴛᴏᴏᴛᴇᴏᴏᴠᴠ ⎯⎯

M aking major changes in the way you live your life and interact with people can be difficult. It can call for confronting fear and taking calculated risks. Sometimes, you just have to keep on ploughing forward despite the difficulties. That might sound a little scary, but the most important step is a relatively simple one: giving yourself permission to recognise those debilitating emotions and reactions and confronting them bravely.

As you saw in "Chapter One: Why We Don't Give OurSelves Permission", many of my clients are virtually paralysed with fear when I ask them what makes them happy. Everybody says that their main goal in life is to be happy, but at the same time, they often have no idea what they need to do to achieve that goal. This can be because they

- worry about what others will think,
- don't want to upset anyone,
- fear appearing selfish or self-centred,
- don't believe that what they want matters,
- don't embrace their own worth, or
- fear failing.

We've looked at why fear gets in our way and why we don't give ourselves permission to think and do what we want, but now we're going to explore ways we can move past these barriers.

Acknowledging Your Feelings

Whatever the origin of people's pain, from outright abuse to a struggle with inconsistent messages, we are all entitled to feel the way we do. When we're afraid, hurt, or angry, we can honour those feelings without giving in to them.

As a young girl, I learned not to express any emotions or opinions. If I did have feelings of disappointment or sorrow, others usually dismissed them or told me to buck up. This meant that I never really understood my emotions, so it was easier to bottle them up. I never completely trusted what I was feeling. As a result, I started to doubt myself and to lose confidence and any feelings of being worthy. It took years before I learned how to give myself permission to understand that I mattered enough to express my feelings.

To move past the negativity associated with some feelings, it's often helpful to verbally express yourself to another person, someone you trust and who will not dismiss you. If you find it difficult to trust anyone at first, try writing your thoughts in a journal – one you can keep safe from prying eyes. Expressing how you feel clears the oppression these feelings hold over you. It's always best to verbalise emotions in a straightforward manner without drama and then release them. Rehashing the issue could just drive you crazy. Ultimately, the aim is to nurture yourself so you're in a safe place to trust and understand yourself. You're allowed to have feelings, and you're allowed to recognise them, but you would be best served to acknowledge them and then let them go.

Learn to Trust

⸻

Remember, you are the only person who thinks in your
mind! You are the power and authority in your world.
—Louise L. Hay

⸻

Safe Fear versus Limiting Fear

Unless we trust ourselves in a truly deep and meaningful way, it's almost impossible for us to give ourselves permission to do anything. There is *safe fear* and *limiting fear*. Safe fear is when your gut instinct tells you something is wrong, like when you think you might take a shortcut through the park on your way home but something tells you that it might be dangerous. It's late, you're on your own, and it just doesn't feel right. Limiting fear is when you decide to not do something because you're afraid to fail, worried about what might happen, or concerned about what others will think. In actuality, you're not taking your desires, needs, and abilities into consideration. Rather, you're allowing your insecurities to dominate you. The challenge is to distinguish between the two types of fear, trust yourself to listen to the safe fear, and recognise the limiting fear as such and push through it. Both responses require you to be brave.

When we have faith in ourselves that we know what's best in a particular situation, with time and practice, we can master the art of trusting others. We can learn to create an environment in which we don't allow doubt to dominate us in the situations we encounter.

Trust Your Gut Instincts

One of the first actions to undertake is to learn how to trust your very basic instincts. Begin by listening to your gut feelings. This starts by giving yourself permission to take that gut instinct seriously. Just like you're allowed to feel your emotions, you're allowed to give weight to what your gut feelings tell you.

If something about a particular situation or decision feels wrong to you, it probably is. I strongly believe that our deep instincts will tell us the truth if we listen to them without prejudice. Often, we know the truth of a situation but don't want to hear it or don't have enough faith in ourselves to take heed.

When I look back, I can see a few instances when I did not respect a strong gut feeling I had. I made decisions that were contrary to what my intuition was screaming at me.

Just before my wedding, everything was telling me not to go to Egypt for the honeymoon. Quite apart from the political instability in the region at the time, my gut instinct and the signs around me were telling me not to go to that region and to go anywhere else instead. I ignored all of it, though. I desperately wanted to go to Egypt, and I didn't want others to think I was afraid or weak. Sure enough, not only did we arrive the day of one of the worst attacks in Egyptian history, but I also experienced my first major MS exacerbation.

Due to plummeting tourism and diminished infrastructure, we struggled to find a flight back to the United States. On top of everything, I was really not feeling very well. If I had known how to acknowledge my instincts and had acted upon them earlier, I cannot help but think that the exacerbation and the accompanying stress may have been less upsetting and drawn out. But I wasn't accustomed to listening to myself.

The Trust Muscle

Different people find different ways of exercising their trust muscle. The key is first to find ways to listen to yourself. This is often easiest in a quiet, calm, and solitary environment. Listen to your body. Is it telling you that you're tired and need to slow down or maybe that you're not getting enough exercise?

If you work in a busy office environment, an easy way to find some personal space is to go for a short walk at lunchtime or even just go to the loo (hopefully no one can get upset with you for that, ask you a question, or follow you in!), lock the door, and take a few minutes alone to unwind, check in with yourself, and focus on your feelings, instincts, and emotions. Ask your body what it's trying to tell you ... and just listen.

Plenty of very successful people practise the art of meditation. Meditation is simply giving yourself permission to empty all of your everyday conscious thoughts, fears, and anxieties so that your subconscious thoughts and answers have room to reveal themselves. We all can benefit from some time and space to simply focus on ourselves and be alone, breathe deeply, and connect with our bodies. You can learn to meditate from many good recordings available in most online bookstores, or you can find a meditation group at your local holistic wellness centre, religious centre, or yoga studio. I've found that the best way for me to get to a place where I can listen to myself and receive signs or understand my gut feelings, is to play some gentle or spiritual music.[7]

An extension of meditation is the practice of visualisation or guided imagery. These techniques are closely related and the terms are often used interchangeably. For me guided imagery is a form of hypnosis and can generally be practised by listening to a recording of someone guiding you to a place where you can achieve peace and relaxation. Many people use a form of guided imagery to stop smoking or promote deeper sleep. Visualisation is when you imagine and see outcomes and success for yourself (we will be doing a visualisation together in just a few pages in "The Letting Go Box" exercise). Amongst other things, both techniques allow the body and brain some space to relax and, in so doing, opens up the mind to more clarity and focus. You can work with a therapist or coach with these techniques or learn more by searching on the Internet for books and CDs on the topics.

It's good to recognise how your body feels when you're anxious and stressed and then when you're happy and calm. When you identify how you physically feel in these states, it becomes easier to focus on transitioning from anxiety to tranquillity. Often all it takes is a few deep breaths, a little focus and some willingness to allow relaxation to enter. When your body and mind are more relaxed, you're much more able to listen to and hear what your gut instincts, and physical bodies are trying to tell you. It can be difficult at first, but it will get easier.

---

[7]   Check out anything by Steven Halpern or Alex Theory or many other New Age artists.

Exercise: Focused Breathing

Right now, right where you are, close your eyes and take a deep breath. Hold your breath for three seconds, exhale to the count of five, and then inhale to the count of eight. Hold your breath, exhale, and repeat a total of three times. If you become light-headed, *stop*, and start breathing normally again.

How do you feel? How long did it take for you to start feeling relaxed? I suspect that it didn't take too long, which should give you an idea of how easy it would be to incorporate such a simple action into your daily life and of what significant benefits it may have.

Seeking Approval

Another way in which we can really learn how to exercise self-trust is to change some of our old patterns of behaviour. For instance, if you've been in the habit of seeking approval from others, try looking to yourself for that approval. This doesn't have to involve grandiose gestures. If you think that your new hairdo or outfit is attractive, trust your judgement and don't rely on the approval of others to feel happy about it. If you choose a new car because you feel it suits your lifestyle and needs, don't look for a thumbs up from your friends or family. Trust yourself to make the right decisions for *you*!

When you master the art of approving of yourself and the decisions you make, you'll reinforce the feeling that you're worth listening to and that your opinions and decisions do matter. When you make a conscious effort to grow your self-trust, you'll find that it becomes even more profound with practice!

A Reality Check

More often than not, it's useful to explore whether our perception of what is going on is grounded in reality or whether it's skewed by our limiting beliefs or past experiences. I call this process a *reality check* and use it with many of my clients as a way to figure out what's really going on in their lives. A reality check is a useful tool that allows us to burst preconceptions, assume a greater degree of personal responsibility, trust ourselves more, feel more at ease with ourselves, and feel more confident. It has positive repercussions at all levels of personal and professional success.

Many times clients who have negative and limiting feelings about themselves or their behaviour will verbally express them to me as an excuse for why they believe they cannot do something. I always challenge them with a reality check.

Clear Out Limiting Beliefs

For instance, clients will make what seems to be a fairly convincing case that they really *are* disorganised or bad at maths or whatever else might be holding them back. Often the belief has been limiting their ability to fulfil any long-held dreams or goals they might have for themselves.

The reality check may go something like this:

"So you say you're disorganised," I would say. "Let's look at the areas in your life where you *are* organised."

"Well," the client might say, "I'm very organised in the potting shed."

"Interesting," I tell him. "This means that you are *capable* of being organised. Let's look at what you're doing in the shed that's working out so well. Why is it easier to be organised in the potting shed than at work?"

The answer might be that it's easier to be organised in the potting shed because he loves working with plants and nurturing the buds and enjoys the physical aspect of this work. In this case, he and I can reasonably conclude that it's more difficult to be organised at work because he doesn't love what he's doing sitting behind a desk *all* day. So, we can problem-solve to learn what he can do to make himself like work more. We may find that he needs to move around more, enhance the creative aspects of his job, or put more focus on nurturing co-workers. As a last resort, if nothing redeeming can be found about the client's job, he may come to the understanding that he may need to find another job, one that he will find more fulfilling. The reality of the matter at hand is that he is *not* disorganised, just uninterested.

Clearing Out What Others Have Said

Other times, I've reached a point where a client says something along the lines of, "I think I'm just not clever enough," or "Maybe I just don't have it in me."

For me, that's another clue to run a reality check.

"Okay," I say when she's expressed a negative feeling about some aspect of her current situation, "can you tell me when you've felt the same way in the past?"

Often, after a little discovery, we end up discussing a point early in the client's life when a relative, teacher, or caregiver said something to her along the lines of, "You're not very good at maths; maybe you should find something to do in life that doesn't involve numbers." But somewhere down the line, the client also heard someone say to a sibling, friend, or classmate, "Oh, look how well you do at maths. You're so clever." The child puts two and two together and comes to the conclusion that she's stupid because she's bad at maths.

Sometimes, we grow up not giving ourselves permission to do things that make us happy because of something someone has said to us. We blame the other person for uttering those cruel, restrictive, and unsupportive words, and we feel our "inabilities" are their fault. At this point, we need to stop and think. What was and is the truth? Who originally voiced the idea that has been holding us back, and could that person have had an agenda? If so, what was it?

Often, it's difficult to discard memories completely, so it can be more productive to change the way you think about and react to feelings or a set of beliefs that were created in the past. It's also useful to attempt to understand what may have influenced the perpetrator. After all, you don't know what happened that might have led the person to say what they did. Maybe another child, a bully, originally created the hurt, but perhaps the bully was acting out because he was getting beaten at home. Maybe the teacher or adult who criticised you was short-tempered because of family problems or illness. We don't know why they said what they did, we never will, and, in the end, it doesn't matter.

Off-hand statements can cause someone to go through life thinking that she's less than stellar, regardless of how much evidence stacks up to the contrary. As a child, she might have reacted by studying really hard in an attempt to prove an unsupportive figure wrong, or maybe she didn't try at all because she felt there was no point. In one case the child may grow into an anxious, driven, perfectionist young adult with low self-esteem, and in the other, she may have developed into an individual with little confidence in her abilities, virtually no pride in her work, and limited personal success. Either way, she has never forgotten the hurtful words that repeatedly play in her subconscious and continue to have an impact on her in the present day.

So, to stack the evidence to the contrary, in a coaching situation like this, my next step is to say, "So what have you done between then and now that indicates that, far from not being very clever, you are actually quite intelligent?"

The answer to this question varies, of course. One client replied that she got a first in her degree from Oxford; another told me that he got his painting business off the ground and profitable in just six months. I have yet to meet someone who isn't able to find an area in his or her life in which he or she has not excelled at some stage. We all have been and are good at something, but we may just not recognise it immediately.

To conclude this part of a session, I say, "There are things that you're good at and areas in which you are actually very clever. What else are you good at?"

When the question is put like that, most people find it relatively easy to recall many of their strengths and times when they've been successful or shrewd or clever. Essentially, I've given them permission to see their strengths and a safe place in which to talk about them. When we go through that process, we can come up with a list and a series of proofs that they *are* clever or they *are* good at doing things after all. This is quite the opposite of what they initially felt to be true.

By walking through this line of thought you can check the reality of a situation, or of the fear you are experiencing, and see the truth of the matter.

Finding and Accepting Reality

In my twenties and thirties, when I thought about my childhood, I would remember how lost, lonely, and small I felt and how difficult I found life. I was confused by the fact that my father was sick and home so rarely, and I was hurt when he left us for good. Looking back, I can see that I felt very disempowered and unsupported. However, that was not necessarily the reality; it was just what I felt and perceived. In our adolescence, we can quickly develop such conclusions from subtle influences.

Even though my environment was slightly unstable, upon reflection I can see that I reacted well to our family situation. I was a strong and resilient child. I now also recognise that I did have support (albeit not always where I expected it or in the form I wanted it) and that I was a very capable child. I worked hard at school and did well, I retained a good relationship with my mother, and I strove to be independent.

In the early days, when my parents had to travel without us, we spent time with our nannies. For us this was a wonderful and enriching experience because we bonded with them and were able to experience a different way of life. I remember going to Yorkshire with one of our nannies and having the excitement of eating fish and chips from a rolled-up piece of newspaper, a meal that was, so far as I was concerned, both exotic and delicious. Heera and I also had boundless opportunities for play dates with the children our nannies' friends cared for. By checking the reality of my situation, I realised that I always had someone around. And I can see that, regardless of how insecure I might have felt much of the time, deep down I *was* happy.

By reality checking, we can understand that whatever people may have said or suggested to us in the past, we are independent, we are clever, we are full of potential, and we can truly empower ourselves. We can let go of old wounds and long-established patterns of thinking and behaving that have restricted our lives – possibly for years. We don't have to fight against or contradict the author of the original hurtful words because there is no need to. Refuse to let a carelessly spoken judgement have an impact on, let alone dictate, the rest of your life.

Of course, there will be times when we reality check our feelings or situations, and discover that, yes, our concern that our own behaviour caused a problem is valid. We may have indeed been hurtful or wrong about something, and we need to take personal responsibility for that and mend the appropriate fences.

We can explore the things that really happened in our lives, accept that they occurred, and move on. Clinging to a version of the past that is groundless or inaccurate gets in our way and makes the present harder to live. Often, reality checking shows people that they're already on the right path in many ways, even if there are areas where they need to make some modifications.

Letting Go and Forgiveness

Sometimes, however, you have been truly hurt. The person who was demeaning or unsupportive was probably misinformed, malicious, or just plain wrong. They almost certainly had no idea what a profound impact their words would have on you as you grew into adulthood.

Although it's sometimes useful to understand why they are displaying negative emotions and behaviours, it's counterproductive to agonise over why people said what they did to you. If their behaviour was clearly wrong, you need to let it go. This is not about them feeling better; it is about you getting some freedom.

We're so often told that we need to forgive others for their actions so we can move on, but I don't necessarily agree with that. I acknowledge that this goes against what many psychologists, therapists, coaches, and self-help gurus say. For many, forgiving someone is difficult or even impossible to do. People feel like they're letting the perpetrator off the hook and, in a way, condoning their behaviour.

When I was getting divorced, I told a close family friend that I hoped one day I might meet someone else. Without thinking, she blurted out, "But who would want you? You're handicapped!" At the time, those words really stung. I now understand this person better and know that she always felt huge pressure to be perfect, and having a seemingly disabling disease is far from fitting into that image of 'normal'. Whilst initially it was very difficult for me to forgive her, in time, I was able to let go of the message, as I understood it had nothing to do with me and, in actuality, she didn't mean it. She was ignorantly talking out of fear. By letting go of the statement, it allowed me to free myself of the hurt and self-doubt.

What I have seen to work for many is to recognise and acknowledge that the action was hurtful and upsetting, attempt to understand why the person said what they did, and what in their background may have contributed to their feelings of inadequacy or defensiveness, and then let it all go: sometimes with love and sometimes just to free yourself of the pain. Many times there is nothing that can be done to change the damaging situation that has already occurred, but there is a way to move past it!

Forgiveness comes with time. It's possible that once you've lived with the freedom of letting those actions or words go, have taken personal responsibility for how you move past them, have lived according to your needs and values, and have created new, more joyful events and interactions, then forgiveness might just happen organically, without you forcing it. I really don't think there's any point in making yourself forgive someone or something in the hope that doing so will eradicate the hurt. Allow forgiveness to happen in the flow of living a unique and powerful life. Eventually, with time and understanding, I was able to forgive our family friend for her thoughtless response.

Exercise: The Letting Go Box

Letting go is sometimes easier said than done, so here's a brief visualisation that may help you. You may find it useful to record yourself saying this visualisation so you can listen to it with your eyes closed as you sit in a comfy chair. Alternatively, because many people don't like the sound of their own voice, you might want to ask a friend to record it. I've made a version available on *www.GYSPermission.com*.

Sit quietly and close your eyes. Take a few deep breaths. Visualise a box. What colour is your box? How big is it? Now think about what you want to let go of. Get a very clear picture of the words or issues, and then focus on the feelings and emotions associated with them. Then pull all those words, images, and feelings out of you and start putting them into the box. Who said the words? What was the situation? How did it make you feel? Now, make sure you get every last one of them in. The box can fit as much as you want to put in it. Then choose a ribbon, visualising the colour, width, and fabric you think would be best to tie up everything you want to let go of, and then tie that ribbon around all four sides of the box and secure it with a big, beautiful bow on top. Know that you've honoured your feelings, but also know that they no longer serve you and will be ceremoniously discarded from your mind and life. Now visualise yourself walking to the edge of a cliff, or if a cliff is too precarious, make your way to a bridge with a safe railing. Now take one last look at the box, think about what's in it, and throw it over the edge. The box could just fall into an abyss, so you never see where it lands but just know it has fallen away forever. Maybe the box hits the rocks below and explodes. Or it could land in the water, bob around for a while, and then be engulfed by the waves, never to be seen again.

Once you are sure you can no longer see your box, walk away from the edge, take a deep breath, and know you are in a safe place full of ease and joy. Open your eyes.

This exercise can be repeated every time you want to honour and let go of an emotion or scenario that no longer serves you.

The Beauty of Resilience

We can use reality checking to determine how resilient we really are. My experience has been that just about everyone figures out that they're much more resilient than they think. When we look objectively at our lives by using reality checking, we can uncover those times when we've been strong and those situations we've recovered from. By figuring out what we did in those instances, we can learn how to use the same sort of behaviour going forward. We can learn how to trust our abilities to tap into our powers of resilience when we need them.

After I was diagnosed, I attended an extremely depressing MS support group. Far from helping people to tap into their reserves of strength and self-worth, it seemed to degenerate into focusing on the negatives – which is unproductive when trying to identify and maintain resilience. For people with a chronic illness – or without one – developing a positive mindset (which we will address further in "Chapter Nine: Give YourSelf Permission to Be Happy") is particularly important for coping with setbacks or making the most of every day. This doesn't mean that we can't acknowledge any anger towards whatever circumstance we have been handed but we must be determined not to let it rule our lives.

A few years back I coached another MS support group. At the time, I made the decision not to share my diagnosis. Whether someone was in a wheelchair or experiencing minimal physical discomfort due to the disease, everyone was a complete, complex individual in need of accepting that they were living a new reality, and each had to find a new way of reacting to it. We worked on how they could lead fulfilled lives and what they could do for themselves. I asked them to list what they liked to do before their diagnoses and what filled their souls? I moved on to asked them what they could no longer do. Each member had the opportunity to share and we then brainstormed, as a group, ways in which each person could modify their previous activities so they could enjoy a version of it now.

By moving the topic of conversation from the illness to that of interests, passions and hobbies, the playing field was levelled, and the group started to see each other as people rather than simply as examples of how a disease can manifest. We moved from a situation in which the less disabled were looking at their wheelchair-bound peers and saying, "I never want to be like you!" and the more disabled were looking at the less disabled and saying, "You are so lucky!" to one in which people could focus on the things they loved doing and how they could find a way to engage in them within the context of their current abilities. By working together, the group came to see that each was very resilient and that this would stand them in good stead as they moved forward. They also realised that they were more alike than different, because all they really wanted was to live a fulfilled and productive life, regardless of where they were on the disability scale. By the end, I was in awe of their bravery. They had opened up to each other, taken risks and been able to alter their judgements.

Growing up, I often felt quite angry with my parents. After all, a situation had been created in which I didn't always feel safe. I had no control over the fact that my father left us. I'll never be happy to have come from a broken family. Yet, at the same time, this was a learning experience with unparalleled opportunities to acquire skills of resilience, self-sufficiency, and maturity. I was thankful for these qualities when I was diagnosed with MS, as I realised that my new reality would be to live with the condition as smoothly as possible for the rest of my life. This resilience, developed earlier in life, enabled me to persevere and find a way to still obtain what I wanted out of life despite a slight change in circumstances! In addition, I was able to let go of all my anger and really embrace my tenacity. In time, I was able to forgive, but most of all, by learning how to look at the situation from a different perspective, I set myself free.

People can give themselves permission to see their own personal strengths every day as they learn to stop judging themselves and to provide that safe place within themselves.

Risk-taking

———⁓⁓◦◦⊙⊙⊙◦◦⁓⁓———

Expand your thinking, diminish your
problems. Increase your love, decrease your
fear. Laugh more, and you'll cry less.
—Marianne Williamson

———⁓⁓◦◦⊙⊙⊙◦◦⁓⁓———

My good friend Steve, who is the CFO of a Fortune 500 company, once said to me, "Priya, whenever I have done something worthwhile, I have always been a little bit afraid before getting started on it."

I think that we've all experienced that fear when we're on the brink of something big. It is scary contemplating change! But that fear can turn into excitement when we trust ourselves enough to acknowledge the emotion and choose to embark on the new journey anyway. I have often been scared of starting something new – even of writing this book – but I have learned how to accept the feeling and dare to do it anyway!

I am not suggesting that everything is always going to be easy and painless once you've embarked on the process of giving yourself permission to take risks. Feeling fear in the face of the unknown is a normal and healthy reaction. It is certainly nothing to be ashamed of.

Fear is instinctive, and we don't need to let it hold us back. We can respect it, understand its role in keeping us safe, and proceed in the new ways of thinking and doing what will help us bypass unrealistic fear and live afresh.

The Risk Equation

Sometimes taking a calculated risk and failing is a good thing, as it increases our chances of real success the next time around.

If we take a risk, then take action, we just might succeed.

Risk + Action = Success (hopefully!)

However, if we experience *failure* then we gain *experience.*

So, the next time,

Risk + Action + Experience = Increased Chance of Success

By using a reality check, you can assess or calculate risks. What would happen if you took the risk and failed? Would you be in the same place as you were before taking the risk or somewhere worse? By asking yourself these questions, you're changing a situation from one of complete uncertainty to one in which you may just want to take a calculated risk.

For instance, if you need to make a sales call or ask someone for something and you're worried about it, ask yourself, where would you end up if you never talk to them? Then ask yourself, where would you be if your efforts or requests were rejected? Most of the time, chances are pretty good that you'll be in exactly the same place. In this situation, after asking and being denied, you'll have gained some insight. You can asses why they said no, what might make them or others say yes next time, and how you can improve your approach. Sometimes an experience like this can teach you that it may be more productive to ask someone else. However, you now have some understanding of the situation (*experience*). Not getting exactly what you wanted, and then learning from it, has allowed you to be one step closer to success the next time. It's important to implement the knowledge you've gleaned from the experience.

Now, if you want to learn to swim and you don't want to take lessons but want to just dive in at the deep end, this may be the time to assess the risk in a different way. What's the worst that could happen? You could drown! Is that worth the risk of learning to swim this way? Failure here would not result in gaining experience because you would be dead, so there would be no way for you to implement the knowledge learned from the experience. Given that the risk of jumping in at the deep end with no lessons or floatation device might not be a good idea, what risk *is* worth taking to attain your goal? What would be a less dangerous risk? Maybe wading in at the shallow end whilst having a lesson with armbands might be smarter at first? Realistically, what is the worst that can happen? You could flounder a little and your instructor might have to help you. What's the best that can happen? With a little practice and repetition, you might just learn to swim like a fish!

This may seem like a very basic example, but it illustrates the point of deciding whether a risk is worth taking because the payoff outweighs the unknown factors associated with the risk or whether the price is too high. I would say that, most of the time, we only perceive risk, and that perception often comes from deep-rooted fears that are not founded in reality. So guess what? Back to the reality check! Bottom line: risks are often worth taking, because we never know what's on the other side or what we just might be able to achieve.

Don't Be Afraid of Success

Sometimes people hold themselves back from being successful because they're subconsciously afraid of what might happen when things go well. I know this sounds ridiculous, and when I say it, my clients balk, as they do when I suggest that people don't give themselves permission to live their lives. We in the psychology and coaching profession see this happen all the time and are sometimes guilty of sabotaging our own success as well. For instance, I had a client, an artist, who was worried about being hugely successful because of the tax implications involved with becoming more profitable. If that happened, he would have to get an accountant and get involved in the system. He held himself back from finding new outlets for his paintings because he didn't understand the tax structure and was afraid of what more money would bring in the way of paperwork.

To help him get over his fear, I suggested he start gaining the knowledge he needed to overcome this seemingly overarching impediment. As it turned out, he wasn't afraid of money but of bureaucracy. He made himself more knowledgeable about the situation and grasped a better understanding of the tax system. Ultimately, he needed to do his taxes like everyone else, and the worst thing that could happen was that he would have to pay more tax because he was making more money, which he was going to have to do anyway if he really wanted to be successful.

As we've seen, people can be afraid of what success might bring. This can be irrational and even subconscious. They might be afraid of being in the public eye and, knowing that a manager will have to do public speaking, they subconsciously sabotage their chances of promotion so that they don't have to do something that they are uncomfortable with. A way around this could be to take public-speaking classes so that they become more at ease in the situation. The key is to deal with the tangible issues rather than worry about the unknown.

The underlying issue or subconscious problem can be almost anything; it depends on the person in question. The solution lies in identifying the fear and addressing it rather than resorting to sabotaging behaviours. This can be done with a good therapist or close friend for some perspective.

Be Brave

———⟋⟋⟋⟋⟋⟋———

Be brave. Take risks. Nothing can substitute experience.
—Paulo Coelho

———⟋⟋⟋⟋⟋⟋———

In conclusion, most of us have things in our lives that we want and need to change. In order to start making these changes, to start on that journey towards a better life, we need to decide what is not working and trust that we will make the right decisions for ourselves given all the information we have. We need to trust that we will be able to make the appropriate changes, and we need to give ourselves permission to follow them through. Nothing is more empowering than feeling brave and being able to confront the situations and emotions that have always been difficult.

There is no point in waiting for the people in our lives to change their attitudes or behaviour towards us, because they're on their own journeys, and we have control over only our own lives and situations. Checking the reality of what really happened in the past and getting some perspective on how you can move forward and let go of what happened can bolster your inherent bravery and resilience.

We tend to live our lives according to largely mythologised versions of reality, and because of this, figuring out what is real, accurate, or true and what is merely our perception about things can be far from straightforward, but not impossible. Keep at it, seek professional help if need be. This kind of work is a lot less laborious and stressful than you might think. For example, the work does not need to be done face to face. Reading books like this or attending workshops or finding online courses can be just as effective. You just have to find the right fit for you.

Taking a risk will usually reap great rewards, but of course, there will always be times when risks don't work out as we might have hoped. Even then, we have gained a learning experience, we have been brave, and we have practised putting ourselves out there and reaching for what we want.

Who knows? Taking a risk and bashing fear on its head may just allow you to be where you want to be and achieve what you want to achieve.

The Permission Journey: Stage 4

So here we are at your fourth stop, in the Canary Islands in the North Atlantic Ocean. You have travelled through the stage of giving yourself permission to be brave in which you explored how to trust yourself, understand the reality of past experience, how to let go of things, and what the benefits are to taking risks. The journey itself is the process – everything you have become aware of, everything you have learned, and everything you have started to implement in your everyday life.

Here is the same set of questions you've seen before, but this time, hold your fears in the forefront of your mind as you answer them. As before, these questions allow you to gauge where you are and what you've learned. As always, it's good to take stock of how far you've come, and your answers to these questions will act as a celebration of sorts. Remember, it's all about taking souvenirs with you and leaving behind items that just weigh down your suitcase.

1) What did you learn for and about yourself in this chapter?
2) What tools or realisations are you going to take with you on your journey?
3) What traits, behaviours, thoughts, or memories are you going to leave behind?

Armed with your newfound sense bravery, you are now ready to embark on the next stage of your journey.

CHAPTER NINE

Give YourSelf Permission to be Happy

People are just as happy as they make up their minds to be.
—Abraham Lincoln

It's Your Choice

Happiness comes from within. This means that you're in charge of your own happiness. Sure, external factors can impinge on your mood, but ultimately, you're in the driving seat and you can take personal responsibility for your mood. When you've created a positive mindset and made the choices that support a positive outlook and create a positive environment, there is no reason you should not make a conscious choice to be happy and make this your default setting. You can decide to perceive things as positively as the circumstances allow. Whatever your age, it is never too late to develop a new mindset that will facilitate living in a different, better way. Give yourself permission to choose happiness.

Somewhere along the way, popular culture seems to have categorised happiness as uncool and less meaningful than darker emotions. Look at how many of the most famous film stars end up in tragic situations or are portrayed as having depth when they act moody. By contrast, people who are unfailingly positive are often ridiculed as being shallow! However, I don't see any good reason why we should buy into the prevailing view that gloom is cooler than happiness.

As children, we cannot help but be deeply influenced by the people we grow up with; however, as adults, we have the ability to seize personal responsibility and actually make real changes. We can effectively alter our outlook on life and decide to be happy.

It's all a mindset, and thus it's up to us to control.

Ed: A Story of Positive Thinking

Ed had had a lot of difficulty at work and in his personal relationships. He hated his job and was constantly frustrated with his co-workers and his family. He had a partner, but things weren't great between them either. Together, he and I figured out a way for him to learn how to think positively. It wasn't easy at first, but relatively quickly, Ed became able to think about things in a different way and to change his perception quite profoundly. He decided to first focus specifically on the things he liked at work. He forced himself to think positively rather than negatively. He started to communicate with others in an encouraging way and to send friendly emails.

Ed had always disliked his boss and was aggravated by her behaviour, but now he looked for and found aspects of her personality that he admired, and he focused on them. He gave himself permission to think positively, which meant letting go of his irritation, anger, and resentment. Interestingly, he started to like his boss more. It became progressively easier for Ed to see her as an individual with whom he could communicate.

The result of all this was that, particularly at work, Ed seemed to be a completely different person than before. His relationships with his colleagues improved, his work productivity increased, and he started to enjoy his life a lot more. He also started taking care of himself and exercising more; this in turn made him more self-confident.

One day, the head of the HR department pulled him aside for a chat.

"Hope you don't mind me saying," she said, "but we've all noticed how differently you have been behaving. And, no offence, but you're a lot nicer to be around than you used to be. We just wondered if you're on antidepressants!"

Shortly afterwards, his company was laying off a third of the workforce, but Ed's contribution had been so valuable, they asked him to stay on. Even so, Ed had figured out that what he needed was a fresh start and wanted to do his own thing. Armed with a new level of self-esteem, he managed to negotiate a ten-month severance package and is now happily running his own multi-million pound business.

Ed was able to transfer his improved relationship skills to his interactions with his family and with his partner. In so doing, his personal life also became much more harmonious.

Tolerance versus Acceptance

Everybody likes to feel that they're in control of their own lives. It can be scary to feel out of control, or that outside forces determine what you do and how you do it. In truth, nothing feels better than knowing that you're in the driver's seat and in charge of your future. So here we look at *tolerance* and *acceptance* and how the later can free us.

There's an important difference between tolerance and acceptance. Tolerance means we put up with something because we think we have to, but we don't like it all and it upsets us all the time. In tolerance the negative stimulus never goes away. We have decided to assimilate it into our emotional landscape without actually accepting it and taking it on board. It will be a burden that weighs us down, as it has a negative impact on our feelings and on our interactions with others. It's like a grain of sand in your shoes, irritating, painful, and more than often damaging.

Acceptance is when we understand that a particular situation might not be great but "that it is what it is". We then must take responsibility for how we react to it. People may be doing things that we don't like or that a certain situations is not ideal, but once we figure out what we can control, what we can influence and what we cannot control, then we must accept the situation for what it is. We cannot allow it to erode our well-being and we must live with the calm understanding that it is not part of who we are, or how we choose to live our lives.

I feel very strongly that if we merely tolerate something, we're not being true to ourselves, and we're potentially causing ourselves great damage by undermining our sense of self-worth. It's my belief that there is no space for simply tolerating things that are making us feel unhappy or unfulfilled.

When I was training to be a coach, all the students were asked to think of a situation that they were tolerating. At first I balked at this concept, as I truly felt that we had to tolerate certain situations and that that was our lot in life. Some things just had to be tolerated. The instructor explained the concept further and pushed me. After gaining some control over my belligerence, I thought hard and came up with something quite silly. As I was living on a tight budget, I didn't want to spend a lot of money on clothes. When I did spend money, it was on the items that everybody could see – that snazzy pair of shoes or a fabulous dress. The result was that all my underwear was grey, stretched out, and had started to get holes. I was tolerating this situation, but it was annoying me and chipping away at my happiness. I had been telling myself that it didn't matter. Who saw my underwear, anyway? Was it not more important for me to present myself to the world by dressing well on the outside?

As insignificant as this problem may appear, I was actually getting pretty annoyed looking at my ratty briefs every day. I decided not to tolerate the situation any longer, threw the old underwear away and bought new items at an inexpensive chain store. They weren't fancy, but at least they didn't have any holes – and I was happier because I felt better about my decisions and myself.

When it comes to the people in our lives, we can also choose to move away from them or to accept them as they are. There is no point in wishing and hoping that others would change, because they are, or should be, in the driver's seat of their own lives. We can support and help them when they need us, but we cannot fundamentally change them. There are people whom we don't want to move away from, like family members, but we find ourselves tolerating them, and that makes us really unhappy. So, at this point, it may be helpful to go back and look at their values and see if we can accept those people because we know they're living in accordance with their values. If we are lucky we recognise that they possess some similar values to our own, and we can nurture our similarities rather than our differences. Sometimes this kind of exploration benefits the situation and sometimes it doesn't, but it's very much worth giving it a go. We might find we can accept a lot more than we would have thought, and, therefore, we can decrease the amount we tolerate and accept them for who they are. In so doing, life will be a lot easier for us.

Making the distinction between situations in your life that you're tolerating and those you've accepted is an important step in eliminating things that are a drain. It's good to understand that tolerating parts of your life that bother you doesn't really help anyone and will ultimately hurt you.

The Art of Positive Thinking

Your own mind is a sacred enclosure into which
nothing harmful can enter except by your permission.
—Arnold Bennett

People who are happy see the world in a clearer, more focused way than others. They make better decisions and function more productively. Like Ed, we must make a choice to see what is positive around us.

You'll experience many benefits in your personal, emotional, and professional when you think positively, and are happy. An important by-product of deliberately choosing to be happy is the ability afforded by your newfound confidence to give yourself permission to live in a way that is consistent with your vision for yourself each and every day.

The merits of positive living are far-reaching and have profound impacts on success, health, longevity, relationships, and more.[8,9]

Learning how to think in a positive way can be tremendously liberating and helpful. And really, who doesn't want to be happier?

Changing Negative Self-Talk to Positive Self-Talk

Often when I meet clients for the first time, I find that they're very hard on themselves. They say, "I am so stupid!", "Gosh, why did I do it that way?", or "There I go again!" They berate themselves for past decisions and hold negative opinions of their overall conduct.

I wonder out loud how they think they'll get ahead when they constantly say such harsh things about themselves? We need to learn to be kind to ourselves. If we don't speak to ourselves positively, how can we expect anyone else to? One of the first exercises I get my clients to do is to make a mental or written tally of each time they say something negative about themselves. When they come back the next session with their list, they're always amazed by how often they feed themselves with negative reinforcement.

The next part of the work lies in either stopping them from uttering or thinking the negative phrase or turning it into a positive one. Instead of saying, "That was stupid of me," they can say, "What did I learn from this situation? How can I do better the next time?" or change it altogether and focus on what they did well rather than what they did poorly.

---

8   Shawn Achor, *The Happiness Advantage: the Seven Principles of Positive Psychology that Fuel Success and Performance at Work*, Virgin Books (2011).
9   Martin E. P. Seligman, PhD, *Authentic Happiness: Using the New Positive Psychology to Realize Your Potential for Lasting Fulfilment*, Atria Books (2004).

Practising Gratitude

One of the most important tools for developing a more positive way of thinking is practising gratitude. I'm not talking about just saying thank you when someone does something nice for you; I'm talking about thinking quite deeply about all the things that you're grateful for, all the things that are positive and encouraging in your life.

One of the best ways to help your mind to tune in to happiness is to learn how to identify the good in your environment. Unfortunately, many people focus on the negatives instead. Practising gratitude helps you see all the many things in and around your life that are good and positive for you.

Some people identify three things that they are grateful for and write them down first thing in the morning. This exercise prepares them to have a positive mindset for the rest of the day. Others do the same thing at night, when they look back at their day and find three things they experienced that they feel good about, providing them with a positive sense of closure. Some families do it over the dinner table so that they can share their experiences of the day in a positive and collaborative manner. These people think or talk not just about what three things made them feel grateful but also why. In so doing, they explore the richness of the experiences and the associated positive emotions. For instance, a lot of people say, "I am grateful for my family." Exploring this in the context of the day in question, they might find they're grateful because they knew they would be at home at the end of the day and looked forward to a lovely family dinner which made them feel loved, safe, and secure.

Whilst many work on thinking positively at specific times of the day and make it part of their routine, I draw out this tool when things get difficult. I think it's a very useful trick to practise gratitude in times of crisis as a way of finding the silver lining regardless of how trying the situation is.

Shortly before I started writing this book, my patience was put to the test. It was the Jubilee weekend, and everybody in Britain was celebrating the sixtieth year of the Queen's reign. I had invited some friends to celebrate with me in my flat. Shortly before they were due to arrive, my one and only loo literally exploded. Great! It was not an easy day, but I gritted my teeth and realised that I would not get through it very well if I didn't find something positive in the situation.

"What are you grateful for in this situation, Priya?" I asked myself.

I thought for a minute or so and came up with a reasonably long list: I was lucky to be living in the twenty-first century. Two hundred years earlier, if I had been living in the same place, I would not have had indoor plumbing and would have had to use a chamber pot. I quickly realised how grateful I was that there was a plumber just a phone call away and that I knew that even if it was a nuisance, unlike in many countries, pretty soon everything would be back to normal and there wouldn't be a problem anymore. Besides, the porter let us use his loo. It took a week for my landlord and the plumber to actually fix the defective loo, but all the while, I held on to the knowledge that it could have been much worse given different circumstances.

When I explain the technique of practising gratitude to clients, I sometimes find that they look at me with some cynicism and say something along the lines of, "Well, isn't that very Pollyanna-ish?" Pollyanna was the young protagonist of Eleanor H. Porter's 1913 novel of the same name. She was the epitome of an optimist. She even made up a game called the Glad Game in which one had to find something one was glad for in every situation.

So when clients are taken aback by having to essentially play the Glad Game, I say that learning how to see the positives, even when things are really very difficult, is one of the most important actions we can take to be happy. I think Pollyanna had a point.

The more we become accustomed to looking for positives, the more we exercise the relevant muscle, and the easier it will be to remain essentially happy.

Change Is Possible

Before we go any further, let me address the myth that it's difficult to change our habits. In fact, our brains have been proven to show physical change with certain stimuli, giving us the potential to alter our outlook and actions. Scientists are only just starting to understand that no matter how entrenched our patterns of thinking are, our brains can still change. Our bodies stop growing when we reach adulthood, but the brain is capable of changing, morphing, reshaping and relearning throughout our lives to suite our needs. This research is called Neuroplasticity, and whilst completely fascinating, it is way too large a field to expand on much further here.[10]

However, because I'm such a Londoner, I just had to share a study that looked at London taxi drivers and the part of the brain that is thought to govern spatial navigation, the hippocampus.[11] London can be very higgledy-piggledy, so taxi drivers need to take a test known as the Knowledge, which can take up to three years to train for and pass. Taxi drivers need to be very good at spatial navigation to get around quickly and easily. The researchers looked at taxi drivers of varying ages

---

[10] Norman Doidge, *The Brain that Changes Itself*, Penguin (2007).

[11] Eleanor McGuire et al., "Navigation-Related Structural Change in the Hippocampi of Taxi Drivers", *Proceedings of the National Academy of Sciences of the United States of America*, vol. 97 (1999).

and experience who had all passed the Knowledge. Interestingly, the veteran drivers had larger hippocampi than their novice counterparts. Specifically, their anterior hippocampus was more developed. This showed that the brain was able to adapt to what it was needed for.

Many people who have suffered from devastating brain injuries can regain many of their abilities. The signals in the brain learn to circumnavigate the damaged areas and find another, different way to enable the person's functions. This shows that not only is the brain capable of acclimating to what we need it for but that it is also capable of dramatic healing.

I once knew a twenty-something man who had had an accident that resulted in a subdural hematoma (bleeding in the brain). He lost some of his vision and had severe issues with his memory. He had to learn to be self-reliant all over again. He started by navigating the street by foot, then by bicycle, and finally by driving again. He lived at home with his parents until he adamantly requested that he get a place of his own. He would stick notes up all over to remind him to turn off the oven or lock the door. He was told he would never go back to university and that he should consider vocational training with repetitive work. He did go back to university and earned his bachelor's degree. He then went on to graduate in the top 5 per cent of his class at a top MBA program. He is now a marketing executive, has started a few businesses of his own, and sits on various philanthropic boards. Who says the brain can't rewire itself?

Many clients start by saying they cannot change, but I tell them that's just an excuse for fear or lack of interest. If the brain can change, so can we. We simply have to commit to change, choose to tune in to the positive stimuli in our environment, and channel happiness as often as we can.

Developing Positive Habits

Over the years we can pick up a few bad or unproductive habits more easily than productive ones. These habits get automatically hardwired into our brains. The good news here is that we can train our brains to hardwire the positive habits as well.

Conventional wisdom proposes that it takes twenty-one days to change a habit.[12] This means that if we want to add a life habit to or subtract one from our routine, we have to start off by doing or not doing the activity for twenty-one consecutive days. In the process, our brain will rewire itself and the habit will gradually either become subconsciously easy or go away.

So, if you want to add a fun activity or an action that will bring peace and happiness into your life, you can consciously do so by making yourself carry it out every day for twenty-one days. Once you've practised this for twenty-one days, it will be ingrained in your mind as the norm. You can do this with going to the gym, practising an instrument, or engaging in any activity you desire. By the end of the twenty-one days, it will be much easier to keep the new habit in your routine.

I decided to address my bad habit of leaving dirty dishes in the sink (my little flat didn't have a dishwasher). I felt really disgusted with myself every time I went into the kitchen and saw a huge pile of mess. I printed out a twenty-one-day calendar, posted it on the kitchen cabinet, and checked off each day after I washed the dishes, giving myself a gold star if I washed up after each meal. Ideally I would have liked to have an empty sink every evening, but that was too much to ask of me. However, as I washed and checked off the days on the chart, I started feeling happier. I started to look forward to having a clean kitchen. At

---

[12] Maxwell Maltz, *Psycho-Cybernetics: A New Way to Get More Living Out of Life* Pocket Books rev. 1989 (orig. 1960)

the same time, something else very interesting happened. I started to be comfortable in the kitchen. I started to cook healthy food instead of just microwaving packaged food. I felt better and I lost weight – just from washing my dishes!

When something starts to go better, everything associated with it will become easier too. It has a trickle-down effect.

Affirmations for Positive Thinking

——~~~◦◦◦◦◦~~~——

We are shaped by our thoughts; we become
what we think. When the mind is pure, joy
follows like a shadow that never leaves.
—Buddha

——~~~◦◦◦◦◦~~~——

Affirmations are specific statements used to elicit positive thoughts. To use them, create a sentence you can come back to that will help you refocus on an empowering mindset. This can be a very valuable tool. Saying aloud something along the lines of "I trust myself to make the right decision for me" can help to solidify the decisions you've made that require confidence to put them into action. Affirmations should be in the present tense and be encouraging, and they need not represent exactly what you're feeling at a particular point in time; they can represent the reality you aspire to rather than the one you're currently experiencing.

For me, affirmations are a great tool when I'm feeling stressed or things aren't going so well. An important one for me is, "I am happy, I am healthy, and I am well." Many people have a similar affirmation that they use when they're feeling out of balance or out of sorts. Make up an affirmation for yourself, and use it like a mantra. I find when I repeat my affirmation over and over again, I calm down and am more able to continue the task at hand. Putting the thought into words can be the first step towards subconsciously gearing your actions towards achieving it.

You can also post these affirmations on your bathroom mirror, on your phone's wallpaper, or beside your bed; you can list them on your computer or in a notebook or journal; or you can put them on flash cards you refer to when you need a bolster. The point is that these are phrases you can make up and refer to whenever you want. If you're having trouble coming up with some, then you might, at first, want to take a look at Louise Hay's *Power Thought Cards*.[13]

Vanessa: A Story of the Dividends of Happiness

Vanessa came in for coaching because she was unhappy with her work situation. A self-employed PR consultant, she found it very difficult to find new clients. She was limping by with a few regular clients but really wanted to ramp things up a notch and start to realise her potential. We worked on developing affirmations that would make her feel more positive and proactive, and literally within a week, she had signed up a new client.

Using affirmations and training the mind to think along more positive lines is not magic. Vanessa came up with the affirmation, "I am good at what I do, and I have clients whom I like working with."

Affirmations opened up her mind and heart to new possibilities, and she primed herself to see and be more accepting of the opportunities that were presented to her.

---

[13]   Louise Hay, *Power Thought Cards*, Hay House (2004).

It's All About Mindset

———✦———

Whether you think you can or whether
you think you can't – you're right.
—Henry Ford

———✦———

In *A New Earth*, Eckhart Tolle[14] describes a scenario in which a driver gets a flat tyre. The driver is already late for an appointment and is immediately annoyed. He has two choices in this situation: either he gets cross and stands on the side of the road cursing and feeling upset, or he changes the tyre and gets on with things. Either way, he knows he's going to arrive at his destination a little late, and there is nothing he can do about that.

When the scenario is put in such a logical manner, the choice seems obvious to me. We can choose to get irritated and upset or to see the problems for what it is, get on with the job at hand, and then move along. We can choose how to approach each obstacle in our path. If we choose to see it as a negative, then it will invariably get us down.

We have to understand and take advantage of the fact that every experience in life, regardless of how difficult, can be a learning experience and that nothing can undo how much we've achieved. We can be grateful for the strengths that we've acquired in the course of our journey. We can also recognise that some of the difficult things we've experienced were not our fault. This is not about blaming but about understanding reality and coming to terms with it.

I'm not here to tell you that every bad thing in your life has happened for a reason, but it *is* important to recognise that we can learn something

---

[14]   Penguin, 2008.

from every experience. Difficult and despairing experiences can teach us as much as positive ones, or at least they don't have to be our undoing.

Each of us lives a unique life that reflects our past and our experience of family and friends. Like many people with a generally absent father, I found that my father's personality loomed large in my life, both before and after he left. I remember being about ten years old and sitting in front of my mother's vanity table while she put eye gel and concealer under my eyes to hide the dark circles. I was upset because I felt as though this meant my mother thought that I was not good enough the way I was. But what I didn't know was that she felt under huge pressure to make everything perfect for my father. She had to be perfect, and so did I. Even after he had gone, the feelings continued.

Whilst I cannot undo this memory or do anything about the confusing dynamics in my family at that time, the experience was a blessing in disguise. I have used eye cream every day since I was fifteen, and that has certainly worked to my advantage. I have fewer wrinkles than most of my peers, and some say I look a little younger than my age! Although the action may have been born out of unhealthy sentiment, once I overcame it, I knew that dwelling on it was nothing more than wasted energy. More importantly, I've turned those feelings of shame into gratitude for my mother's actions.

Mindset is constant choice, and it's a personal one. At first you'll consciously have to switch from a negative one to a positive one. In time, you'll see that having a positive mindset is fun and much more peaceful, and thinking this way will become automatic.

Exercise: Make a Playlist

Nothing speaks to our emotions as strongly as music. A fun way to engage with your emotions and switch your mindset or mood to a more productive, positive, or relaxed one is to make a playlist of songs and music that capture the mood you want to experience.

If you want to relax, make a soothing playlist that will allow you to drift off somewhere. If you're going out and want to overcome any nerves or shyness, make a playlist with fun, upbeat, and empowering tracks. Which song first comes to mind for you? I might choose Shania Twain's "I Ain't No Quitter". Playing music can quickly help switch your mindset and give you a way of accessing self-made empowerment at any time.

The playlist can be as highbrow or as cheesy as you like; no one but you need listen to it. I rather embarrassingly like world-renowned classical music conductor Bobby McFerrin's 1988 hit "Don't Worry, be Happy".

If you go to *www.GYSpermission.com*, you'll see a few of my playlists, and you can add yours if you want to share them.

Give YourSelf Permission to Have Fun

Do you sometimes think, "Well, I just don't have the time to have fun," "I don't want to seem silly and frivolous," or "Having fun makes no money"? And then what happens, do you have fun anyhow, or negate that side of you?

Now consider how you feel after having had a little fun, a good laugh, or a let-it-all-hang-loose dance. What is your mood like at this point?

How does your body feel? What do people say about you? Generally, I suspect, you feel lighter, calmer, and maybe freer. I know I do. People might also point out how good you look and be attracted to your spirit and energy.

So why do so many refuse to give themselves permission to have fun, or feel guilty about it? Many people feel that having fun is a waste of time or that they shouldn't be taking the time out. Also, in the conventional workplace, having fun is seen as goofing-off or as being unproductive. Increasingly, however, many of the new companies, especially technology companies like Google and Yahoo!, have come to see that it's good to encourage play and, in fact, it increases productivity. Prospective employees are told on Google's website that fun and play are an integral part of their company's culture and a component of their success.

I cannot tell you how many clients look at me blankly when I ask them what they do for fun. They have no idea, and when pressed to come up with something, they squirm in their seats and often show real resistance to giving themselves permission to even think of doing something for themselves. This is when I ask them to tell me what they used to do for fun when they were younger, less busy, and had fewer responsibilities. Generally they can remember something, a flicker of recognition crosses their faces, and they visibly relax. Let's take a look at Jack, whose story we saw in "Chapter Five: Give YourSelves Permission to Know You Matter". You'll recall that, after much probing, he remembered how he used to work with his father in the shed and how much fun it was. Even though his father was no longer around to share his time and hobby, Jack could modify the activity, and still get great pleasure out of it.

Exercise: Fun

What did you used to do that made you happy? Something that was a lot of fun? Is there an element of whatever it was that you could take and blend with your current lifestyle? What would the activity look like now? What actions would you need to take to make this fun activity happen? What small changes might you have to make? So, are you willing to give fun a go and not feel guilty about it? Are you ready to take pleasure in the action alone and recognise how it makes you feel? What do you hope to get out of having more fun? Many find they're far more productive at home and work after having had a little fun and are more engaged with those around them. So, why not go out and have some fun?

Don't Worry, Be Happy

—⊱⋆⊰—

We tend to forget that happiness doesn't come as a
result of getting something we don't have, but rather
of recognizing and appreciating what we do have.
—Frederick Koenig

—⊱⋆⊰—

Life is simply more enjoyable and much more peaceful when you make the choice to focus on the positive. By looking around you for what is good and what you are grateful for, you will find it easier to make healthy choices for yourself. You'll be more fun to be around, and you'll attract friends and colleagues who enhance your life rather than take away from it. It's also very useful to choose the freedom of acceptance over the acid of tolerance. At first, it might seem quite challenging to change your mindset to a predominantly positive one. You may find it quite difficult to recognise when you speak to or about yourself in a negative way. But once you catch yourself, the goal will be to stop in your tracks and change that negative thought or comment to a positive one. You might have to force yourself at first, but a positive way of thinking will lead to higher self-worth, self-esteem, confidence, and, ultimately, a firm foundation for you to springboard into the life you dream of.

The Permission Journey: Stage 5

You have now arrived on top of the world at the Franz Josef Land archipelago in the Arctic Ocean. You have travelled through the stage of giving yourself permission to be happy. Here, you've had a little fun and explored how to change your mindset through gratitude and positive self-talk. The journey itself is the process – everything you have become aware of, everything you have learned, and everything you have started to implement in your everyday life.

Here is the same set of questions you've seen previously, but this time, hold your mindset in the forefront of your mind as you answer them. As before, these questions allow you to gauge where you are and what you've learned. As always, it's good to take stock of how far you've come, and your answers to these questions will act as a celebration of sorts. Remember, it's all about taking souvenirs with you and leaving behind items that just weigh down your suitcase.

1) What did you learn for and about yourself in this chapter?
2) What tools or realisations are you going to take with you on your journey?
3) What traits, behaviours, thoughts, or memories are you going to leave behind?

Armed with your newfound sense of happiness, you are now ready to embark on the next stage of your journey.

CHAPTER TEN

Give YourSelf Permission to Have Healthy Relationships

———〰️◦⊶❦⊷◦〰️———

Nobody can hurt me without my permission.
—Mahatma Gandhi

———〰️◦⊶❦⊷◦〰️———

What Is a Healthy Relationship?

Deep down, we all have the power and knowledge to understand and decide what a healthy relationship is for us. Depending on our roles, we have a different relationship with each person in our lives. Hopefully, we have different relationships with our mothers than with our partners, different relationships again with our children and with our best friends.

You can choose what you want each relationship to look like, what you can be responsible for, and how each of these relationships fits into your life. Admittedly, this can be difficult at times, such as when your father is being unreasonably hard on you or your children are fighting in the back of the car and there's nothing you can do about it at the time.

In this chapter, we'll explore how you can shift your perspective in terms of how you view others and how you can change your behaviour to achieve outcomes you want and the healthy relationships we all need.

First, you need to decide what a healthy relationship looks like and entails. For me, for instance, a healthy relationship with my mother is one in which I am not angry with her, where we can love each other unconditionally, and I accept her views about my life (and sometimes the things I'm doing) not as an affront but as a statement of what she holds to be true and valuable for her – whether I agree or not. I need a relationship in which I am not trying to change her and in which I feel able to be who I am and make the right choices for me. In general, a healthy relationship for me is one with open lines of communication and mutual, balanced, and beneficial respect and support – not to forget fun!

Exercise: What Does a Healthy Relationship Look Like?

Take some time to think about and outline what a generally healthy relationship would look like for you. Write it down and use it as a road map much as you use the list of values you drew up for yourself. Look at all your existing and new relationships and see if the qualities you've outlined are present in them.

What Needs to Come First?

———————————

As we let our light shine, we unconsciously give other
people permission to do the same. As we are liberated
from our own fear, our presence actually liberates others.
—Marianne Williamson

———————————

By now, keeping the Permission Journey in mind (outlined in chapter three), you should be better able to believe that you matter and that if you take care of yourself and understand your values first and foremost, you're much better able to help and communicate with others in a healthy way. You've stopped blaming others and have taken responsibility for your life and everything you think, feel, and do. You've understood what you have control over and what you don't. Now you're in a position to start seeing the best ways in which to interact with the people around you.

You've looked at your own fears, tried to take a few risks, and learned to be open to seeing what's really going on in your life rather than letting your perceptions overtake reality. You've learned how to trust yourself so you can start learning how to trust others. We've explored how to seek the positive at any given time so that you can change your mindset and therefore start seeing the good in the situation and the people around you.

All this culminates in giving yourself permission to understand your relationships, accept what they truly are, and decide if you need to give yourself permission to change the parameters of certain relationships or even make the hard choice to end a few.

So let's see how to get to this place of choice.

Don't Compare Your Insides with Everyone Else's Outsides

Often, we look at the people around us and think that they have it better than we do or that they've been given more advantages in the form of privileges and luxuries than we have. We might have feelings of envy, which can be damaging, undermining, and insidious and can only function to make us feel bad about ourselves in the long run.

When my former husband and I first met, he gave me one of the best pieces of advice I have ever received; I have never forgotten it, and I am often grateful to him for his wise words.

"Priya," he said, "don't compare your insides with everyone else's outsides."

I think that we've all found ourselves comparing what we *know* about our lives to what we *think* is going on with the lives of others. Often we look at their outsides and assume everything is great without considering that there just might be a whole other layer of thoughts, insecurities, hopes, fears, shortcomings, health issues, pain, abuse, wishes, or desires that they don't share with everyone else. When we compare ourselves to all of their glitz, it's easy to see ourselves as coming up short. We look at celebrities or business tycoons, school friends or relatives and think that they've achieved so much more than we have.

"She has got it all," we think. "She must be so happy!"

But what's *really* happening?

I suspect most people looking from the outside would have considered my family circumstances pretty much perfect, but, as I've already shared, the apparent fairy tale was quite inconsistent with the confusion we experienced behind closed doors. I rather begrudgingly felt that there were times when people thought, "Oh, the Kapoors have it all!

Mum is young and glamorous; Dad is so sophisticated and handsome. Their children are lucky to be growing up in such a cosmopolitan, exciting environment!" In some respects we did have an adventurous life, but it was difficult.

Maybe your successful boss at work *does* sit in his fancy corner office all day long and go home at the end of a productive working day to his good-looking, happy wife and children, but perhaps he really wants to be doing something else entirely. Maybe he has high blood pressure from working long hours, constant fights with his wife, and exhausting kids who run riot all evening. Who really knows?

It's important that we see that we can only truly understand *ourselves* and that we need to focus on bettering our own lives rather than fixating on others'. With this understanding comes the recognition that, ultimately, we can only learn how to be really happy when we learn how to take personal responsibility for how we live and what we have control over.

The simple fact is that we just do not know what is going on in most other people's lives. The only person you will ever know completely, inside and out, is yourself.

Communicating with Others

—⁓◦◦❧❦◦◦⁓—

How people treat you is their karma;
how you react is yours.
—Dr Wayne Dyer

—⁓◦◦❧❦◦◦⁓—

We've already explored identifying and understanding how important our core values are. As we grasp the centrality of our value systems, it should become easier to understand that others' values are just as worthwhile to them! This includes family members, friends, colleagues, and everybody we interact with. Whilst we will never completely share another person's values, we can work hard to respect them and have regard for their position in that person's life.

As we gain clarity about our own values, we have a much better chance of identifying others' values and communicating with those people within their respective value systems. We can respect that they each have a value system just as we do. If we honour our own value systems and know that we do not want others to try to change them, we should extend the same courtesy to the people around us.

Understanding and appreciating that the important people in my life may not live completely according to the same values as I do has been tremendously freeing. Now, I know that others simply live according to their personal value systems and that within those parameters, they've done the best they can – just as I try to do, according to *my* values. Just I am personally responsible for my life, they are responsible for theirs.

When we understand others' core values, we learn to identify and respect people's actions. Perhaps autonomy is one of your core values and you know which behaviours are associated with it. You can see it in others and are therefore better able to be respectful of others' need for autonomy. However, sometimes you don't understand someone's behaviour or recognise his or her values. Sometimes people talk about values being good or bad, but they are only good or bad in relation to something else. *Good* and *bad* are matters of individual perception and, often, judgement. Judgement is fine as long as you resist imposing it on others.

Your boss may put great value on being dominant, whilst you like to take a back seat and succeed quietly. You both get to the same place but choose different routes to reach it. You really don't like his outward appearance of bravado, so you think and feel that his value of dominance is bad because it makes you uncomfortable. In reality, it is *his* value; it keeps him safe and comfortable, just as your values do for you. So how can you relate to him and demonstrate that you understand his value system? Maybe try communicating with him in a direct, clear, and powerful manner. He just might understand that method and will be able to productively respond to you. In time, as you attempt to express your values to him, he may start communicating with you, keeping in mind your subtle, peaceful, and quiet communication preference. Just as much as he is more likely to feel valued by you, he may also be more likely to hear you and possibly communicate with you in a manner that you find more comfortable because he feels listened to. Neither of you need to change who you are, but you can each modify your communication styles to make them compatible.

Understanding others' value systems is especially important when it comes to the central relationships in our lives, those with our partners, spouses, and closest friends. How can we have a healthy relationship with someone we care for deeply unless we understand and can work within his or her value system?

When I was growing up, I often heard my mother talk about relationships and marriage, and what would constitute a good job. For her, social standing and financial security were very important. I know that the often bold statements came from her past experiences, but at the time they really annoyed me.

I soon started to think that my mother and I might just not prioritise our values in the same way, and maybe we might not have all the *same* values. However, that didn't stop me from worrying that she didn't approve of my decisions. It also meant that I put myself second and tried to live according to her value system. This essentially confused and paralysed me. But now that I've started making my own values a priority and living in accordance with them, I am no longer trying to live her life, which was not authentic for me. Instead, I am living *my* life. As a result, we have a much healthier relationship.

By understanding that others' perceptions, judgements, and values belong to them and have nothing to do with us, we can set our angry feelings aside and focus on making the necessary loving changes to our relationship.

Respecting Others' Agendas

Something else to keep in mind when communicating with others is the understanding that everybody has their own agenda. I do, you do, and all the people in your life do as well. So, when we seek permission from others to do the things we want, is it fair to expect them to be able to give perfectly objective advice? They are always going to give advice with their own understanding, which may be right for them but may not be so good for us.

When we don't consider ourselves worthwhile, we tend to seek approval from others, but it may not come in the form we want or need. We need to be careful that when we seek approval, we're prepared to get it not on our terms but on someone else's.

To take a trivial example, you might have a pair of smart jeans and want to wear them out. You try them on and ask a friend, "Do these jeans make my legs look short?" Maybe the answer you're looking for is simply no. You love this particular pair of jeans, and you really just want confirmation that they're great and that you look fantastic. But what if the person you're asking favours an honest answer and tells you that yes, your legs do look short in those jeans? When we look for approval, advice, or input from others, we have to be prepared for it to be on their terms. Sometimes it will be helpful, but it could also not be the answer you *wanted* to hear.

As we explored in "Chapter Nine: Give YourSelf Permission to Be Happy", it's crucial to view things in a positive light. This also goes for how we look at other people. I am not immune from making hasty judgements. There was a time when I looked at strangers on the Tube and made silent conclusions about them. I don't like those large earrings that make a big hole in the earlobe, and I often thought, "How ugly! Why is he deforming himself like that?" In the end, though, it's absolutely none of my business. Who am I to judge and assume that my values and my aesthetic sensibilities are better than someone else's? His earrings are not interfering with me in the slightest, and they are the wearer's own way of expressing something about himself.

Exercise: Shift Your Perspective

When you travel on public transport, stand in a queue at the cinema, or go to your local bar, try to find someone whose appearance would usually ignite a series of negative judgements from you. It might be someone who happens to wear shabby clothes or who is of a different race, creed, or colour. It doesn't matter; we are all vulnerable to making negative judgements at times. Judgement comes from a place of fear or misunderstanding. Now look beyond the aspect of their appearance that triggers your negative thoughts. Find something nice to say to yourself about them. Maybe you might notice their lovely smile, or think, "Look how tender he is towards his mum," or "Aren't her nails well manicured?" or whatever you need to think to reframe your thoughts in a positive way. Bear in mind that as you look on them with judgement, they could be doing the same to you! This is a great exercise because it can be done in any situation and at any time. As well as teach you to be more accepting of others' values, it will help you work on tuning in to a more positive mindset every day.

Leslie: A Story of Seeing the Good in a New Boyfriend.

———⟶⟶⟵———

If you do not like something change it; if you can't
change it, change the way you think about it.
—Mary Engelbreit

———⟶⟶⟵———

My client Leslie was divorced. She had grown up in a family of addicts and was quite on edge around anyone who showed signs of defensive, selfish, or self-centred behaviour. When she detected these signs, she would get angry and walk away without giving the other person a chance or try to shame them into changing their behaviour. She and her partners were invariably unhappy, and all her relationships broke down.

Leslie was starting to think that she would never be in a romantic relationship again and that that would be all right. Then she met a man who, because of his past addictions, was a prime candidate to exhibit the traits she didn't like. However, this man had some self-awareness and really wanted to work on himself and his recovery. In contrast, Leslie found herself always anticipating the worst and soon realised that she was projecting her anxious and negative feelings, preconceived ideas, and past experiences onto him and the outcome of the relationship. This made for another strained partnership.

At this point Leslie decided that she needed to break this pattern of behaviour and that she was going to focus on the good things her new boyfriend was doing for her and the relationship. Instead of running away at the first sign of what looked like trouble, she decided to embrace the good and trust herself to wait and see where the relationship went. If it became unhealthy, she would do what was best for her. As she had worked with a therapist and was then in coaching, she decided to exercise her new skill of being grateful for the positive in this relationship. She started to see that her boyfriend was trying; he was aware of his traits and was able to listen to his sponsor and others in his therapy group and take on board what they said. He didn't get defensive when she expressed some of her own feelings and reservations about particular situations or their relationship as a whole, and he tried to be mindful of them.

Leslie felt less anxious about the relationship because she was savouring the things that were good in it. She was able to recognise what she wouldn't tolerate and accept what she could. In recognising the positives, she understood that there was a lot more she could and wanted to accept. This made for a healthier situation because she was also giving her partner space to make mistakes and recognise changes he needed to make for himself. All of this allowed them to build a stronger, healthier relationship together.

At work or in our personal relationships, we often focus on that which is going wrong and how others offend us when we're unhappy. Instead, focusing on others' positive behaviour and traits can help to create a healthier view of the relationships in our personal lives and at work. People don't usually go out of their way to offend us; we just see aspects of their behaviour that we don't like because these are always easiest to spot. If we start looking for the things we *do* like, life quickly becomes more manageable. Focusing on people's achievements and likeable traits can change how we view situations and can allow us to communicate and live with everyone much more harmoniously.

As we saw in Ed's story in chapter nine in which his co-workers thought he was on anti-depressants just because he decided to see the positive in people and his work, looking at the good in people can help us see opportunities available to us just as much as looking at issues and events in a positive light can.

Childhood Baggage

———ᘯᘓᘓᘓ———

There is an expiry date on blaming your parents for steering you in the wrong direction; the moment you are old enough to take the wheel, responsibility lies with you.
—J. K. Rowling

———ᘯᘓᘓᘓ———

As we've discussed in various contexts, we all carry baggage from our childhoods and early lives, no matter how supportive and caring our parents may have tried to be. Most parents do their absolute best with the situations they're dealt with and the information they're afforded.

We all grow up in a social environment composed of parents or guardians and often siblings and extended family. We pick up messages about what our place in the world should be from how members of this group treat us and respond to us. Inevitably, these messages contribute to the adults we become; to our strengths and weaknesses, to how we view ourselves, and to our behaviour. Our backgrounds and the people we care about have a huge impact on how we relate to others and how we make the decisions that shape our lives.

Traditional psychology[15] teaches that we take on certain characteristics in our family of origin in order to live harmoniously with our parents and siblings. One child might play the role of the 'protector' by endeavouring to always be one step ahead of all the others to anticipate mishaps. Another might play the role of the 'scapegoat', the hapless or naughty one who never seems do anything right, who acts up to get attention, and whom everyone blames when the family appears to be off balance.

As we grow up, our roles in life change, even in relation to the same people, and the characteristics that once defined our roles may no longer serve us. As we try to have adult friendships with our sisters and brothers or become responsible for our ageing parents' well-being, roles are reversed and old patterns of behaviour will not nurture or support these new roles. Similarly, we will enter into intimate relationships, and we can't always treat our partners as we did our family members. They just may not want to be controlled, babied, anticipated, blamed, or whatever the case may be! If we behave towards them as we learned to interact with others as children, we may fail to create a relationship that is sustainable.

From my rather interesting childhood, I learned a number of behavioural patterns that stemmed from how I believed I stood in relation to the other people in my life and to what I thought they wanted or needed from me. From early on I saw my mother as someone who was rather fragile. When life got tough for us, her response was usually to throw a party. This was her coping mechanism; it was her way of finding strength in difficult situations. For her, being surrounded by friends and fun was a way to survive, and she genuinely thought that her children wanted and needed the same. I now know it could have been worse and she always did the best she could do given the information she had at the time.

---

[15]   In particular, family systems theory, or systemic theory, as it's known in the UK.

At a very young age, the message that I received from my mother was that she wanted *me* to be the person who would be available to pick up the pieces for her and be a fabulous party hostess by her side. I went to great lengths to smooth her path and make her life easier. I developed a habit of anticipating her every move so that I could do as much as possible to make the outcome of every situation more comfortable for both of us. I knew that it wasn't my fault that my father had left, but I also thought that my mother couldn't take care of herself and wouldn't be able to manage if I didn't do whatever I could to help out. Admittedly, she expected a lot of me, but maybe not quite as much as I took on. In reality, my mother has a larger-than-life personality. She wanted me by her side, and I perceived this as pressure, whether it was intended as such or not. However, the foundations were being laid for me to become a strong, self-sufficient woman, whether I realised it or not.

I meet a lot of clients for whom being strong is very important. Often, in conversation, it turns out that they have had to become strong because, for one reason or another, their parents or caregivers were not able to be strong for them when they were growing up. This could be because of the parents' personalities or simply because of unfortunate circumstances – maybe one of their parents was ill or was physically or mentally frail. People who have lived through a terrible situation, such as violence of some sort, when nobody in the family was safe also tend to attempt to control the circumstances around them.

Someone who is battling with characteristics learned in childhood that are no longer healthy or useful *could* blame their parents or extended family members for not encouraging them to develop other healthy traits, or they could blame themselves for not taking the reins and riding off into their own lives. We can always find fault somewhere, but what's the point of belabouring the issue?

It's time to pick up those reins and steer ourselves towards healthier interactions. We now need to give ourselves permission to stop living the historical roles that may be expected of us. To put it simply, it's time to raise ourselves, and it's time to grow up.

Trusting Others to Make Their Own Choices

As well as learning how to trust ourselves, we need to master the art of trusting others. This is quite difficult because if we get it wrong, we run the risk of getting hurt. I think that many of us, for one reason or another, find it difficult to trust others because we don't live with trust, even of ourselves. We consistently think and feel that life is out to get us, as our past experiences have shown that life can be difficult, unpredictable, and often unfair.

When you feel this way, it's time to carry out a reality check: make a list of all the times when people have been trustworthy and what you've learned or gained from the experience. This inventory will start you on the path of recognising that you don't need to distrust every person and every situation. Just be careful not to gloss over any of their obvious or dangerous shortcomings. You don't want to make excuses for bullies or abusers.

When you look at your list of the trustworthy friends, do you see any patterns? For instance, do you see that certain school friends are trustworthy but those you went to university with are not? What does that say? Maybe you should put your trust in your school friends and not your university friends. It's all about knowing who to trust and why, given the situation at hand.

Interestingly, many of us have spent years running around doing things that are intended to make others' lives easier. However well meaning these actions, the fallout from them is that we're giving the clear message that we don't trust them to make decisions for themselves. We may be trying to help, but what we're really doing can actually be disempowering to others *and* to ourselves.

It's important to learn how to trust others to make important decisions about their own lives, just as we make decisions about ours. We don't have to withdraw from the people we love – we can still be there for them when they need us, and we can offer our advice when it's asked for – but we need to trust that they'll be able to take care of themselves. When the outcome of their decisions is not what we would have wanted for them, we must accept that it's not our responsibility. In the end, who are we responsible for? Our children when they are young, for sure, or our dependents with intellectual disabilities or dementia. But, anybody else? If we take over someone else's role of making decisions for themselves, are we really helping them?

We often encounter people whose happiness is dependent on that of someone else. This is known as being *co-dependent*. This essentially means that they are only happy when everybody around them is okay. If they perceive that another person is upset or angry, then they are unhappy and upset too and will only be happy when they can change the other person's mood. This can be a losing game. Learning how to trust and value ourselves makes it easier to understand that our personal happiness does not have to depend on that of others. If we don't let others live for themselves, we're effectively taking learning and experience away from them. Such a person can lose all sense of personal responsibility.

Of course it's important to care about others, and of course it's good, normal, and natural to rejoice when things are going well for the people we care about, but placing all our happiness in the perceived well-being of others is good for nobody. I have met mothers whose happiness is utterly bound up in that of their children and their husbands. Things get difficult when the children grow up and become independent or when their husbands have to be away on trips. Often, it's not enough for family members to tell these mothers that they're happy; the mothers have to *see* them being happy. I've also met working parents who struggle with guilt about not spending enough time with their children. They often overcompensate by deciding that if they can't be at home all the time, they'll be the ultimate parents when they are available. Between work and parenting, they allow almost no time and space for themselves or their children's independence.

How Our Behaviour Affects Others

—————ᴡᴏᴏᴏᴇᴛᴏᴏᴛᴏᴏᴏᴡ—————

And as we let our own light shine, we unconsciously
give other people permission to do the same.
—Nelson Mandela

—————ᴡᴏᴏᴏᴇᴛᴏᴏᴛᴏᴏᴏᴡ—————

I've seen many people reach a stage at which they start to feel that time is running out to address the lack of satisfaction and fulfilment in their lives. They reach the point where they feel they might not survive unless something changes. Even when we understand why we don't give ourselves permission to do the things we want to, it can be hard to get beyond that realisation to reach a point at which we feel empowered to make real change in our lives.

People are often afraid to change the way they behave towards others, as they worry that they'll upset the apple cart and, as a result, damage their personal relationships, possibly irreparably. When we consider change, we often worry about upsetting the status quo of our family's or social circle's dynamics and assume, with reason, that those around us won't welcome that change.

In families and in other close-knit groups such as communities or workspaces, each member plays a specific role, and all of the roles are interlinked. I liken this to a game of chess; each piece can only function in relation to all the other pieces. Move one piece and everything alters because you've changed the status of the game. By taking responsibility for our own lives, we subconsciously stop taking on responsibility for others' lives. It may not be easy at first – it probably won't be – but over time, focusing your responsibility on yourself and how you interact with others rather than on fulfilling the role you assume is expected of you will make a huge and very positive difference in your life, and by extension, in your relationships.

This could feel odd at first but, in fact, taking care of yourself and making healthier choices about your own behaviour is far from selfish. You'll face challenges and might come across people who are angry with you because you've changed the game. Perhaps you always said yes to your sister no matter what and you no longer live like that. She may be angry that you've stopped "supporting" her. I would urge you to remain focused on the matter at hand, which, as we've explored, is sweeping your side of the street.

In time, in letting ourselves take personal responsibility, we often find that others start to be more open to taking personal responsibility too. When real change happens, the effect can be almost magical. For instance, the parent who has long leaned on his adult child for support and help in every little matter will realise, when this behaviour is no longer being supported, that he is much more self-sufficient than he thought. This happens because, on some level, most people instinctively know when the interaction within a family or another group does not work, and they realise they have to step up and do something about it. When the discomfort is too great, people are forced to make change one way or another.

In my family, I gave myself permission to look at my behaviour and how it was impacting me and those I loved, and I made a conscious decision to change things to support myself and allow others to live their lives on their own terms. At first it was really difficult, as no one understood what was happening to me. I felt they thought I was being selfish and mean, and maybe sometimes they did. But in the long run, there were some very positive ramifications for how we all interacted. My sister and mother now get along much better, and we all listen to and support each other much more, as we're no longer trying to control or change one another. Luckily, it seemed that as I evolved, everyone else did too!

The Choices We Make

We all have to make important choices about how we interact with the people in our lives. Do we walk away from them? Do we stay? What kind of relationships do we want to have?

James: A Story of Friendship

A client of mine, James, told me how disappointed he was with an old friend.

"I'm always there for him as a friend," he said, "in good times and bad. But he seems only to want to hang out when I'm up for some fun. I feel that I'm the one putting all the effort into our friendship and that Mike wouldn't bother with me if I was having a bad time at work and was being a bit of a downer."

We talked about this relationship, and James realised that he had been tolerating his friend's behaviour for years without accepting it and changing his own behaviour in relation to it. Mike's behaviour annoyed him, but he hadn't done anything about it. Eventually, he determined that he could either move away from the friendship and decide that it had run its course or accept that his old friend was great fun on a night out but not the one to turn to in a crisis. He decided to accept the latter and to look elsewhere when he needed practical and emotional support. Mike would always be fun when he wanted to go out for a few pints or to a football match but was not someone to lean on emotionally. Once James had decided to accept this as okay, he could let go of his anger and resentment about Mike's behaviour. After all, Mike was just living by *his* values, which were in some instances different from James's.

Be in Healthy Relationships

When it comes to healthy relationships and taking back our own lives, how we define what we want in our relationships is up to us. So long as our needs and desires don't depend solely on someone else changing, we have every right to work on creating these relationships by taking control of what we can, letting go of what we cannot, and understanding where our actions can influence outcomes.

Now, whilst I know you have it in you to make the changes you need to in your relationships, as we have seen, it is not always going to be easy. There will be times when it is downright hard and when the people in your life are resistant, at least at first. It can be isolating, and it can be lonely. But my message to you is that trusting yourself and allowing yourself to be who you really are is feasible, it is doable, and it will make positive changes not just for you but for everyone you care about.

The Permission Journey: Stage 6

So here you are at your sixth stop in the Maldives, in the Indian Ocean. To get here you learned what it takes to be in healthy relationships. The journey itself is the process – everything you have become aware of, everything you have learned, and everything you have started to implement in your everyday life.

Here is the same set of questions you've previously seen, but this time, hold your relationships in the forefront of your mind as you answer them. As before, these questions allow you to gauge where you are and what you've learned. As always, it's good to take stock of how far you've come, and your answers to these questions will act as a celebration of sorts. Remember, it's all about taking souvenirs with you and leaving behind items that just weigh down your suitcase.

1) What did you learn for and about yourself in this chapter?
2) What tools or realisations are you going to take with you on your journey?
3) What traits, behaviours, thoughts, or memories are you going to leave behind?

Armed with your newfound communication skills, you are now ready to embark on the next stage of your journey.

CHAPTER ELEVEN

Give YourSelf Permission to Know Your Dream Team

———~ww•o•◡✦◌•◠◡✦◠◌•◡•ww———

I am successful today because I had a friend
who believed in me, and I didn't have the heart
to let him down. —Abraham Lincoln

———~ww•o•◡✦◌•◠◡✦◠◌•◡•ww———

This chapter introduces you to the concept of the Dream Team.
There are three different types of Dream Teams:

- Your Foundational Dream Team
- Your Current Dream Team
- Your Inspirational Dream Team

And not to overlook *You* as another's Dream Team member.

Why am I mentioning teams amid all the talk of encouraging you to take
personal responsibility and determining whose life you're living? You
might be thinking that you're now all alone and that you have to go it
alone – but, of course, that's not true. I believe that we all have many

more supporters than we might think! Your team could include a tutor you had at university or a teacher in school who saw your potential in a particular area and encouraged you. Remember the story I told in the prologue about my old boss Joe who came to visit me when I was sick? Well, he is almost certainly the captain of my Dream Team. His action made me feel like I mattered to someone. Sure, I mattered to many people at the time, and I probably knew it, but all of a sudden, I *felt* it. Joe's attention and presence came from a place of love and was uplifting. He changed my life. Without him, I probably would not be here doing the work I'm doing today or writing this book.

Your Foundational Dream Team

The rung of a ladder was never meant to rest
upon, but only to hold a man's foot long enough to
enable him to put the other somewhat higher.
—Thomas Henry Huxley

When I was training to be a coach, my class was asked to write a list of a hundred people who could help us with our business in some way. "Yikes!" I thought. "One hundred people?" I wasn't sure I even knew a hundred people. I persevered and came up with a pretty decent list, and this started me thinking about all the people over the years who had supported me.

Making a list of your Foundational Dream Team is an extension of the gratitude concept we discussed in "Chapter Nine: Give YourSelf Permission to Be Happy", as it involves scanning our environment for the positive. The people on this list should be the individuals who have offered you strength, who have inspired you, and, dare I say it, those who have given you permission to be yourself. These are also people who have encouraged you, given you a chance, seen your potential, and been willing to help you. People who have been there in both small and large ways.

The point is, we are not alone. We do not have to face life's challenges alone (nor should we leave others on their own). It's enriching to be grateful for the sparks of wisdom and visionary words that come our way, sometimes from the most unexpected places. Some people's input can be incredibly valuable, but we also have to critically decide what advice we choose to take.

The concept of a Foundational Dream Team was born out of the list I was encouraged to make whilst in my coaching programme. A few years ago, I was feeling quite low. I had recently moved back to the UK, I was struggling to start my business, and I had just left a relationship that I had been quite invested in. I had neglected to make new friends upon my return to the UK, and as a result, I was feeling alone. I needed some outside encouragement, but I really didn't know where to turn. I had a handful of amazing friends in London whom I had known since childhood, but I felt there were only so many times I could lean on the same individuals. I decided to take matters into my own hands and take some responsibility for my own self-esteem and self-worth. I also knew I had to recognise the many things I had to be grateful for to help change my mindset.

So, having remembered the list I had made of one hundred people who could help me in my business endeavours, I decided to write a list of all the people who I felt had believed in me in the past. I wasn't sure how many I would come up with, but as I wrote and the list got longer and longer – I was amazed and humbled. As soon as I remembered one person, another would pop up, and so on and so forth. Some of the people on my list were individuals I had worked with, others were doctors who had taken care of me, teachers who had believed in me, family members who had been there for me, friends who had loved me, and pastors who had soothed me. I was then able to see my relationships in a new light, and I didn't feel quite so alone.

Not everyone on your Dream Team has to utter life-transforming words at crucial moments in your life. Some can be people you may have met only once or twice, and many probably don't even know that they played an important supportive role in your life. When we see people who believe in us, we feel worthwhile. As a result, we feel better about ourselves, our self-esteem grows, and we can then make healthier decisions for ourselves.

Again, this kind of work is to be done for our insides, for our own private use. I have never shown that list to anyone – that might be bragging and conceited – but it makes me feel good inside and encourages me to keep engaging with people in the best way I know how.

I remember a particular talk I had with my neurologist. He had been my doctor for over eight years at this point, so we knew each other well. I confided that my then husband and I had decided we probably didn't see a future together and were thinking of separating. He responded by saying, "Whatever you do, Priya, make sure that you have an enchanted life."

Those words resonated with me, and I've tried to live by them ever since. I was so captivated by his words that they became embedded in my value system. He's a member of my Foundational Dream Team.

Some Foundational Dream Team members have helped in a physical way but often don't understand the impact they've had. I remember very fondly a cobbler I finally found who helped me fix my shoes in a way that helped relieve my back pain. I will be forever grateful to him for his kindness and persistence. He made a fundamental difference in my life by doing his work in a compassionate and thorough manner and contributing to my physical well-being.

A client of mine told me about a member of her Dream Team, a florist who worked on the street near her home when she was in her late teens. She was walking home one day, distraught, as she had just broken up with her boyfriend.

"You look like you could do with some flowers," the florist said as she passed, and he handed her *five* bunches of chrysanthemums! She was amazed that he had even noticed her and that he had shown her such kindness. It made the feelings of loneliness and hurt more manageable and gave her faith that she would be happy again. She is now in her forties and still remembers how he made her feel, and I dare say he has no idea what a difference he made in her life.

The people on your Dream Team may have worked for you or vice versa. They might know that they're important in your life, or perhaps they don't even remember who you are. Whatever the case, they were the ones who were willing to reach out and lend a hand when you needed it.

Knowing that there were people who cared about you, believed in you, and felt that you were worth some of their effort, and your own, is one of the most powerful tools that you can have in growing your sense of worth and, ultimately, in learning how to give yourself permission to do what you think is right and best for yourself. The key lies in recognising them for their efforts and the seemingly small yet often profound impact they had on you. The act of making this list can be eye-opening and extremely encouraging. So, who are the people who have changed your life, who has believed in you in some way or really helped you without knowing what an impact it would have on you? Who has gone out of their way to be kind to you?

Unfortunately, sometimes people give up their whole lives for others. They feel constantly drained and often grow resentful and unable to see those who added to their lives. This is not because they're being purposefully ignorant but because the pressure to be there for everyone else overwhelms them. These distracting blinkers don't allow them to even recognise any kind of positive attention from others.

You may find it difficult to identify your Foundational Dream Team members, or you might say you don't have anyone. But I would challenge you to think deeper. I'm sure that you'll be pleasantly surprised by the result.

I wrote my list in my phone. I sometimes take it out to remind myself that people have cared in the past and that I owe it to them to keep going and make them proud. It is the motivation I need to give myself permission to continue trying to do my best every day.

When I said that I wanted to make them proud, I was half joking. By identifying these people, we're not only practising gratitude and taking stock of the fact that we just might be worth something, but we're also in some way making ourselves accountable to these individuals. If they felt we were worth their time, then we need to honour their efforts. It's sometimes easier to be accountable to others at first, as it exercises the muscle of accountability before we learn and want to be accountable to ourselves. It's a little trick we can play on our brains. We can practise what accountability feels like. We can then face the real test, take personal responsibility, and understand that being accountable to ourselves can also be sufficient motivation to live our lives to their fullest.

Your Current Dream Team

———ᴡᴏᴏᴇᴛᴏᴏᴛᴏᴏᴡ———

A friend is someone who understands your past, believes
in your future, and accepts you just the way you are.
—Author Unknown

———ᴡᴏᴏᴇᴛᴏᴏᴛᴏᴏᴡ———

Many of us get stressed and exhausted because we think that we have
to do everything on our own. Speaking for myself, I still shudder when
I remember the days when I thought I had no choice but to do my own
accounts. All my life, I have found everything to do with numbers and
money very difficult. It used to make me so nervous that I just shut
down. I think my anxiety around money came about because of the
childhood I had, with the uncertainty about resources and the fact that
I was not as good at maths as my school friends.

Years later, bookkeeping became an awful chore that ate into the time I
had available to work with my clients. Eventually, I realised that I needed
to hire someone to help. I resisted the notion for a long time, as I felt I
couldn't afford it, but I finally gave in. Well, the results were amazing.
Not only does Matthias do a much better job than I ever could, but I
have more time to devote to the work I love to do. I also realised that I
had been subconsciously blocking new clients from coming in because
I feared the additional paperwork that would inevitably result from
seeing more people. By now, I have wholeheartedly embraced the
knowledge that this lovely German man is a very important member
of my Current Dream Team!

I would encourage you to make a list of everyone you know who is
around to help you in some way; this is your Current Dream Team. Each
of us has a Current Dream Team, even if we haven't yet learned how
to think of our relationships in that way. Nobody can do everything on

their own. Of course, I pay my bookkeeper for the service he provides, but many of the members of my Current Dream Team don't provide a paid service, and most of them don't know that they're on my Dream Team in the first place!

Exercise: Who's in Your Current Dream Team?

I do realise that not everyone can afford to hire help, but your list can be comprised of people you pay and who you do not pay. Either way, these people help you in a small or large way. The point here is to be grateful for them and know that you can go to different people depending on their skills and the agreement, said or unsaid, that you have with them.

When I did this exercise for the first time, I focused on who could tell others about my business, who might be able to spread the word. However, let's look a little further. Your list could include the cleaner in the office who stops everything from descending into chaos, the friend who loves you enough to tell you when you're being unreasonable, the sibling who never lets you forget your mother's birthday, or the colleague whose eye for detail complements your ability to see the big picture. There are many people who are unaware of their importance to you, such as the friendly old man in the corner shop who sells you a Danish every day on the way to work and whose warm "good morning" always cheers you up. These people can be on your Current Dream Team too! They don't have to know it – the fact that you know that you have such a long list of people who support you in their various ways is what really matters here. You are not alone.

This exercise is useful on multiple levels. First, as mentioned, it helps us practise gratitude and therefore keep a positive mindset; second, it gives you a list to go to when you might need help with something but can't think of whom to ask off the top of your head. Sometimes you'll realise that someone may have a contact you hadn't considered.

As we discussed in "Chapter Ten: Give YourSelf Permission to Have Healthy Relationships", not every person is appropriate for every instance in which you may need help. You may have a close friend who's great at setting you straight when you go on a wobbly but who you would never go shopping with, as she doesn't have the same style as you. Different people can help you in different ways. However, all people on your list should be trustworthy. As we've seen, trust is a big issue and can get in the way of asking someone for help and, indeed, of any relationship. Last, this list will help you identify a group of people who have similar values to yours and, in some way, have your best interests at heart.

You might be thinking, "I don't want to ask people for help all the time!" I'm not suggesting that you do. What I am saying is that sometimes knowing there are people available is good enough. Granted, you have to pick and choose who and how often you ask for support, but this list allows you to make more informed and focused choices if you do ask for help. The thing is people don't have to say yes; it's up to them to choose. However, in my experience, people generally want to help others as long as they don't feel resentful or taken advantage of.

Again, sometimes it seems easier to be accountable to others for your actions and dreams, but ultimately you are only truly accountable to yourself. You can take strength from knowing that there's a Dream Team behind you and that throughout your life there have been so many people who believed in you. But just as you need to learn how to give yourself permission, you need to learn how to be accountable to yourself. This means that you live your life according to your own standards. It does not mean being hard on yourself, but it does mean taking personal responsibility for your actions and honouring yourself accordingly. Even the most important members of your Dream Team cannot be tasked with giving you permission to do what you want and need to do.

Your Inspirational Dream Team

—————————

Leaders don't create followers, they create more leaders.
—Tom Peters

—————————

Have you ever seen a quote you thought was just great and that really encapsulated how you felt about life, or one that reflected your life or work philosophy perfectly? Did you think you might want to be like that person or might want to know more about them?

Exercise: Who's in Your Inspirational Dream Team

One of the best ways to be successful is to learn about how other people did things and tweak those actions to your own style. You might say, "Well, that flies in the face of 'don't compare your insides with everyone else's outsides'," but, in fact, it does not. I'm not asking you to compare yourself to others; I am suggesting that you look at people you might think have done something worthwhile or something you might want to do and learn from them. Research their childhoods and life stories; learn from their mistakes, strategies, and successes. Thankfully, most successful people have published some sort of biography or memoir. Identify a handful of people, maybe five, who have inspired you in some way or who you think have done a particularly good job with something, and find out a little bit more about them. Alternatively, if you don't want to read a whole book, a little Google search will go a long way. Now write down all the traits you admire. See which traits you share, identify the ones you need to work on, and get to work! Again, all of this can be done without anyone knowing. Sooner or later, though, the game is going to be up: as you start to care about yourself and become empowered and inspired, you'll change the way you do things, and you might just be noticeably happier.

I've been an Apple Mac user since the dawn of time, and I have loads of Apple products, so when Steve Jobs's biography came out, I immediately read it. I had heard rumours that he wasn't the easiest of people to deal with, but I had enjoyed his products for many years, and they had made my life a lot easier, more enjoyable, chic, and fun. Sometimes I think I may be hardwired into my music! When I read his biography, I learned some very important lessons. I learned that he had a habit of just getting things done, right then and there. He didn't run things by committee and hence didn't slow things down with deliberation. He assumed responsibility for the product. Admittedly, he could do this because Apple was essentially his company, and he was the driving force behind it.

Of course, not everyone heads a business and can make all their business decisions without clearance from others, but we *are* all the bosses of our lives. Steve Jobs's biography taught me that sometimes I don't have to wait to ask people if they think it's a good idea for me to do something. I can give myself permission to do what I think is the best move in a given situation.

Streamlining Your Dream Team

Don't walk behind me; I may not lead. Don't
walk in front of me; I may not follow. Just
walk beside me and be my friend.
—Albert Camus

In recognising the immense support that a Dream Team can provide,
we need to be careful to distinguish between support and permission.
Whilst the members of our Dream Team provide us with the ability to
ask for practical help and advice whenever we need it, we, however,
need to avoid looking to them for absolute permission. Taking personal
responsibility means that we are our own ultimate granters of permission.

So, let's delve into this a little further. My mother is on my Dream
Team. However, like many people, she is not a blanket member – she's
good for some things and not for others. As I've said repeatedly, I spent
many years seeking her approval and permission. If she did approve of
my choices, then I felt she was happy with me. Because of this way of
thinking, I often ended up doing things to make her happy which did
not make me happy. In so doing, I hadn't taken personal responsibility
for my life, and I had lost all hope of giving myself permission to do
anything I thought was best for me. I had orchestrated a situation in
which there was just no space to give myself permission to be me!
So, my mother is not always who I turn to when it comes to making
emotional choices; however, she is absolutely the first person I would
go to if I were ill, in an accident, or had to go to the hospital. She is
tenacious with doctors, and I know that she would do anything and
everything to make sure I had the best care and that I stayed alive. I
know she loves me beyond measure, and I have no doubt that she

would have my back in a life-or-death scenario. She's also a good lunch and shopping partner, but not a great workout buddy!

Be sure to make a close inventory of all your Dream Team members and assess whether you're looking for approval from any of them. You can ask their advice as long as you're not looking for their validation in some way. The right advice from the right person can go a long way; after all, we're not experts in everything. However, it's up to you to make a decision for yourself given all the information you can gather.

It is virtually impossible for any one person to be everything to anybody. No one can fulfil every one of your needs. This is why we have different Dream Team members. However, sometimes an individual has believed in you in the past, is currently around to support you, and truly inspires you. This is rare, but you are extremely lucky to have that person in your life if you do.

Lastly, many people believe in some higher power, such as God, Allah, Buddha, or Krishna. Maybe he/she/it can be on any or all of your Dream Teams. You get to choose how you interact with this unseen but powerful force and energy. This is a deeply personal choice and relationship, and it is for you to engage with as you see fit.

You as a Dream Team Member

If you have knowledge, let others light their candles in it.
—Margaret Fuller

At the same time as taking stock of those who have helped us, we need to seek opportunities to put our own positive influence back into the world.

Here comes the twist. I've spent the better part of this book telling you to look within, trust yourself, listen to yourself, and do what you think is best for you. But now I'm going to ask you to consider helping other people and to think about where others might need help. As discussed in "Chapter Ten: Give YourSelf Permission to Have Healthy Relationships", we don't live in a land without other people. We have to interact with others at the same time as taking care of ourselves. So, let's take a look at a way we can help others that is aligned with our highest values and is beneficial to everyone, a way that will not render you exhausted and depleted.

Take a look around and see whose Dream Team you can be a part of. Right away, I know that you'll probably think about your immediate family or all the people you have selflessly helped in the past, people who may have taken advantage of you. Maybe the idea makes you balk, but as we discussed in "Chapter Ten: Give YourSelf Permission to Have Healthy Relationships", you get to engage with people on your own terms because you want to, not because you feel you have to. You get to decide what you're responsible for in a relationship. If it's important to you to make your sister happy on her birthday regardless of what a pain she can be all year round, why not do something nice for her? Be her Dream Team member, and maybe she'll learn from your generosity. Or maybe not! Lead by example; treat people the way you want to be treated without losing yourself in the process.

So what kind of interaction with others is good for you or in line with your values?

As you've seen, some of my highest values are communication, beauty, and being of service to others. One of the ways I can fulfil these values is to stop and ask a lost person if they need help finding something. I live in a part of London where a lot of tourists always seem to get lost. Thankfully, I speak a few languages. When I'm in an area I know well and I see someone looking perplexedly at a map and the street signs, I love to stop and help. At first, the tourists seem shocked and confused or even afraid, but then they soften when they realise I don't want anything from them. After my help, they're usually exceptionally grateful and walk off with smiles on their faces. This makes me feel very good, as I've communicated effectively and I've been able to help someone to navigate my wonderful city with a little more ease. London is a city that I love and hope they do too, so I don't want them going home with a bad impression of London and Londoners. I realise that this might sound really weird, but I know how appreciative I am when someone helps me in a city I don't know. When that happens, I have a more favourable impression of the inhabitants of the city and the city itself, and I'm relieved to be a little surer that I'm not lost and that I'm going in the right direction. I feel more confident, so I'm happier. I would like to think that I'm on the tourists' Dream Team and hope that my intervention helps them.

So whose Dream Team could you be on? As in my example of the tourists, people don't necessarily have to know that you're on their Dream Team. It's really up to them to figure it out. Have you ever smiled at someone and found them shocked at first before they softened, smiled back, and said, "Good morning"? How do you think you made them feel? What you've been doing is spreading positivity and happiness.

When Strength Is a Weakness

What we all need to understand and take on board is that asking for help is emphatically *not* a sign of weakness; it is often a sign of strength. We should not have to wait until we are on a ledge, either literally or metaphorically. Knowing when we need to look outside ourselves, and maybe even outside our immediate circles of family and friends, for help and support is strong and brave. It can also be the first step towards a better, more fulfilled future. Even if the problems we're facing seem relatively small, it's never weak to ask for help.

So many people honestly believe that they have to be strong all the time and that they shouldn't seek assistance from others. Way too often, these people end up spiralling into depression because they don't let themselves voice their feelings of loneliness or anxiety. Feeling increasingly unsure of themselves, they don't want to interact with others, and they retreat into a very closed space that they don't share with anyone.

Many people fear being seen as weak. They worry incessantly about what others will think of them if they let their happy, shiny image slip, even for a moment. They won't give themselves permission to reach out and ask for help. They voice the often erroneous thought that they're a fraud, that if they show themselves too much to others, people might see through them. Most of the time, these are all just fears.

I had no option but to ask for help, and now I can see that this was a time in my life when I was strong, not weak. I remember sitting on that ledge and feeling hopeless, but I listened to my gut, or maybe even a higher power, and I knew I couldn't do it alone. This was a time when I found strength in reaching out to the *right person* and asking for help and support.

Know Your Dream Teams

All in all, it's incredibly empowering, humbling, and comforting to take stock of the people who comprise your three Dream Teams. It's also often useful to feel accountable to them until you get to a place where you can think you matter enough to be accountable to yourself. In one way or another, those people will always be important in your life, and it's important to be respectful of their time and effort.

When you give yourself permission to know you matter, you will understand, and act upon the mutually compatible truths that you alone have the power to make the right decisions for yourself and that you will know when you need to turn to someone from your Dream Team for support and guidance! And last, you'll see that you enhance others' lives when you are a functioning and healthy member of their Dream Teams. Support them, but don't do everything for them, and certainly don't help others to gain approval for yourself. Be there for others when you want to, and come from a place of love.

The Permission Journey: Stage 7

You have arrived in the Balleny Islands in the Southern Ocean. You met your Dream Teams – those people who have believed in you and those you can trust. The journey itself is the process – everything you have become aware of, everything you have learned, and everything you have started to implement in your everyday life.

Here is the same set of questions you've previously seen, but this time, hold your Dream Teams in the forefront of your mind as you answer them. As before, these questions allow you to gauge where you are and what you've learned. As always, it's good to take stock of how far you've come, and your answers to these questions will act as a celebration of sorts. Remember, it's all about taking souvenirs with you and leaving behind items that just weigh down your suitcase.

1) What did you learn for and about yourself in this chapter?
2) What tools or realisations are you going to take with you on your journey?
3) What traits, behaviours, thoughts, or memories are you going to leave behind?

Armed with your newfound sense of support and accountability, you are now ready to embark on the last stage of your journey. From here, you get to go home. This stage of the journey will amalgamate everything you've picked up along the way and add a few last-minute tools. You are now in a place where you can give yourself permission to dream big and live *your* life at home, with your friends, family, job, and hobbies.

CHAPTER TWELVE

Give YourSelf Permission to Dream Big and Live Your Life

Dreams are renewable. No matter what our age
or condition, there are still untapped possibilities
within us and new beauty waiting to be born.
—Dr Dale Turner

Definition of a Dream

It's imperative that you understand what your dreams are before you strategically outline and work towards your goals. People often restrict themselves when they're asked what their goals are, as they feel they can only aim for the things that are currently possible or that are deemed rational by society. Dreaming is a much more creative process than goal setting. It enables you to reach beyond what is currently within your grasp and to aspire for more. In time, you'll learn how to create a framework of goals and actions that will ultimately support your aspirations.

The word *dream* has various definitions on *Dictionary.com*. The ones that I see as relevant here are:

- a visionary creation that stems from the imagination
- a strongly desired purpose
- something that fully satisfies a wish

I think these definitions are incredibly inspiring, and I hope they give you permission to come up with fanciful, genuine, imaginative, and substantial dreams of your own.

Why Is Dreaming Big So Difficult?

Many people don't feel that they're worth the lofty ambitions they sometimes allow themselves to imagine. Often social pressure, fear of appearing selfish and arrogant, fear of being disappointed, or even fear of being blasphemous can get in the way of leading a fulfilled life. However, learning how to dream big is *hugely* important. Expressing and having confidence in yourself can provide you with a colourful vision of a fulfilled and purposeful life.

Not knowing how to dream big is often the single most challenging issue my clients face. People work with me when they're feeling confused or stuck about work or personal issues. They know they want to make changes, but they don't know how. When I ask them what they like doing for relaxation or distraction or what might make them happy, they're quite often stumped. They have a vague idea of what they would like to have, for many that's financial security and success, but they can't visualise what that *looks* like. Issues stemming from our cultural backgrounds, personal lives, and families of origin frequently stand in the way of attaining our goals. There are many cultures in which it is seen as inappropriate to be overtly ambitious and in which having a big dream is considered ostentatious. Perhaps you come from a conservative culture, where doing anything out of the norm is frowned upon, or maybe the only thing standing in your way is your own trepidation.

Sure, dreaming big is easier said than done. Practically without fail, I discover that many of my clients find it quite self-indulgent to dream big and often think they're being greedy to ask for too much. I used to feel that way too. We often think that since we're seemingly so lucky in life because of everything we have and do, we have no right to dream for more. We compare ourselves to others and their misfortunes. Whilst we should always be grateful for what we do have and be cognisant of others' needs, this should not preclude us from planning for our future, and a good one at that. If we *are* in a fortunate position, we are much more able to help those in more difficult places. Being of service is one of the greatest gifts we can give others and ourselves, as long as we don't sacrifice our needs in the process.

Sometimes, religious beliefs raise more questions. I used to think it was very un-Christian of me to ask God for anything for myself. I cannot tell you the number of times I've heard, "Well, if I verbally express my dreams and desires, I'll be tempting fate and something bad might happen." Over time, though, I've realised that we can be comfortable dreaming big when we come from a place of love, joy, hope, compassion, and understanding for others and ourselves, and God just may not mind.

Last, but certainly not least, many don't let themselves dream big because they're understandably afraid of being disappointed. This is a very common human fear. The pain of this feeling is really debilitating, but the truth is that disappointment is a product of our perception of a certain situation. We can choose to look at an event that didn't go the way we wanted it to as a failure and disappointment, or, as we've seen, we can learn from it. In a situation where you're afraid of not succeeding in your dream, it might be useful to assess what would happen if you *did* dream big. What would you gain by having a fun dream and taking a few risks to reach it? What could you lose? Even if things didn't work out, would you have fallen behind your current situation? More often than not, you have everything to gain, and in the worst case, you'll have had a learning experience. If you look at any event and explore it from another angle and alter your mindset to that of a more positive one, I am pretty sure you will see something good come of it. You'll also see disappointment magically evaporate.

The Foundations of Dreaming Big

—————ᴍ◦ᴏᴄᴙᴏᴄᴋᴏᴏᴍ—————

People do not decide to become extraordinary.
They decide to accomplish extraordinary things.
—Edmund Hillary

—————ᴍ◦ᴏᴄᴙᴏᴄᴋᴏᴏᴍ—————

Experience has shown me that it is much easier to dream big once you

- believe in yourself and your capabilities;
- identify and understand your values;
- take personal responsibility for everything you think, feel, and do;
- face and overcome your debilitating fears;
- develop a positive mindset;
- experience healthy interactions with others; and
- identify and develop relationships with those who support you and with those you can support.

These are the tenets of the Permission Journey. Hopefully by this time you've gained some understanding and mastery of these concepts.

By addressing these, you've built a foundation on which you can give yourself the space to dream big, trust your instincts, and take a few risks.

As I mentioned at the outset of the book, I'm not here to suggest you do anything too wild just yet, but I would like to see you reach the stage at which you can start dreaming about the really big important things you would like to do in your life. In addition, consider what you aspire to contribute to your family, the community, and the world at large. This crucial step of dreaming big can trip people up, but even if you initially stumble, the road will eventually become even, and you'll soon find sure footing.

Part of dreaming big is to continue exploring what feeds your soul: what you enjoy doing and what fulfils you. Give yourself permission to walk the walk. Find like-minded people; brainstorm with friends, family, or co-workers; and be open to learning from others. Expand your knowledge on a subject that inspires you by doing research and going to lectures and conferences. Take the back seat if you're nervous, but be encouraged by the knowledge that you're working towards getting off that train wherever and whenever *you* want. Equally, you get to map your specific itinerary.

Exercise: Your Big, Fat, Hairy Dream

Your Big, Fat, Hairy Dream is a fun coaching exercise I use with some of my stuck clients. It's all about opening yourself up to creative and imaginative thought. The idea is to set aside all your presuppositions, assumptions, and self-imposed limitations and to figure out what you really, truly want from your life. All you have to do is sit down and let your imagination run riot. In your wildest dreams, if you could live anywhere and do anything, where would that be and what would you be doing? Sometimes when I do this, I break the dream down into categories such as work, family, home, and hobbies.

Whilst on my coaching course, we had to explore our own big, fat, hairy dream. I realised that mine was to own a Titian masterpiece. Now, realistically, that is probably never going to happen. For one thing, Titian didn't create very many paintings, and they're all in museums or on church walls. For another, they're now worth so much that I don't think any individual could ever buy one! But by setting my sights high, I was able to see that I really like creative, evocative, and elegant images, and therefore I knew I wanted more art in my life. I understood that spending a little money on original art to make my living space more beautiful would be worth the investment!

The big, fat, hairy dream is a simple exercise, but it can be very powerful. I have worked with a man whose job took him all over the world but whose big, fat, hairy dream was to own and relax in a large garden. Exploring this aspiration, he realised that what he was really expressing was a desire to settle in the beautiful English countryside and that he was tired of hopping from one international airport to another. He didn't leave his job but instead worked on establishing a series of goals that would ultimately lead to his return to the UK and would allow him to obtain his ideal country house and desired lifestyle. He put in place a road map for how he was going to advance through his company to a point where they would transfer him back to England. He also started positioning himself to change companies if all else failed.

The people I meet as a coach often have difficulty giving themselves permission to live the lives they want and subsequently also find it hard to dream. By making the dream a big, fat, hairy one, the exercise becomes more like a game, and it's easier to engage with. Some people can access their dreams through pictures, others like to talk them out, and some might browse the Internet. Whatever you do, allow your mind to wander and your gut instincts to guide you.

Whose Dream Is It Anyway?

―――᠆ᜧᠬᢇᠣᠷᠣᠷᠨᢇᠣᠬᢇᡡᡐ―――

If you don't design your own life plan, chances
are you'll fall into someone else's plan. And guess
what they have planned for you? Not much.
—Jim Rohn

―――᠆ᜧᠬᢇᠣᠷᠣᠷᠨᢇᠣᠬᢇᡡᡐ―――

Often, our dreams aren't what we previously assumed them to be. Many of us are handed a set of standard dreams on a plate by our families or cultures. There's nothing wrong with these dreams per se, but we need to be sure that the dreams we hold are really *our own,* and that they are an authentic expression of what we truly want for ourselves. If you had asked me in my early twenties if I wanted to live the sort of settled life I thought was appropriate, I would have said yes. And yet even then, when I envisioned myself in the future, I always saw a lot of travel and speaking and meeting all sorts of amazing people, a lifestyle quite at odds with what I thought I wanted then.

So what about you? If you could do, be, or have anything, what would it be?

Exercise: Vision Boarding

Vision boards can be so fun to make, useful, and often very enlightening. Simply put, a vision board is a poster-size collage of images and words that depicts the vision you have for your life. It's not an arts and crafts project. I encourage many of my clients to use this technique to access the dreams they sometimes find difficult to articulate verbally or in the written word. The vision board is the end product of an intuitive and creative process that can be enjoyed and referred to when you need focus or encouragement. I don't think there is a right or wrong way to create a vision board; it's an individual project, and you need to find a way of approaching it that works for you. Here's an example of what works for me; you can adapt the exercise to match your own needs.

The key to creating a good vision board is to be open to whatever comes up, trust your instincts, pay attention to the creation process, and have fun. And remember to dream big! Don't limit yourself by thinking too small.

Step 1:

Develop a clear idea of what you want this specific vision board to represent. For example, it might represent your dreams about who you want to be, where you see yourself living, what contributions you see yourself making to the world, your life, or your family's life – right down to the dream of writing a book, starting a company, having your own blog, travelling the world, or climbing Mount Everest. Just by making the board, everything that needs to happen for you to make your dream come true may well reveal itself.

Step 2:

Choose three or four magazines you think are interesting and relevant to your dream. Don't think too hard; just pick the ones that jump out at you. Even if you don't usually read magazines, the benefit to using this medium is that there's a random element to it. Unlike an Internet search in which you consciously direct your research, choosing an image that catches your eye can throw out all sorts of useful surprises. The final step in the preparation process is to *pick up a coloured poster board.*

Step 3:

Go through the magazines and freely rip out the pages with images, titles, and quotes that speak to you or evoke some positive or empowering emotion or feeling. Keep your focus on your dream. Again, don't think too hard, just keep ripping; you can always sort later. I suggest doing this in one sitting to get momentum. You'll know when you have enough material.

Step 4:

Find and **add anything imperative to the board** that you didn't find in the magazines, such as a specific number, date, or image salient to your dream. I needed a book outline image for mine. These can often be found online.

Step 5:

Cut out everything you found from the ripped-out pages. Examine what you chose to see if anything surprises you or if a pattern emerges.

Step 6:

Firmly paste the images onto the board, starting with a picture of yourself in the middle. I sometimes find the larger images can anchor the corners, and then smaller images can overlap the larger ones. It's most beneficial to do this in one sitting, but take your time. You'll start to see themes and groupings, and you can paste related images together. Do what makes sense to you.

Step 7:

Admire your work, focus on what you really want, and gain a general idea of what your actions need to be to make your dreams come true. Some of the images will evoke a feeling or thought for you but may mean something different to others – don't worry, it is *your* board and you can show it to or hide it from whomever you please.

Vision boards can be used to help clarify all sorts of issues, such as planning for a new year with January or your birthday as your starting point. They can also be used to articulate visions for a new career or project, starting a family, joining a new group, or whenever you feel the need to clarify or focus on something.

The Pitfalls

*Whenever you take a step forward, you
are bound to disturb something.*
—Indira Gandhi

It's not uncommon for someone who has just begun taking responsibility for him- or herself to find the experience a lonely one. We can all be participants in the blame game, and to be the sole family or group member to initially wear the mantle of personal responsibility can be quite isolating. I have seen people whose efforts have been met with outright hostility from onlookers. The fact is the game has been changed on the other people, as they were quite happy being in control. A lot of their initial resistance relates to their inability to understand what's going on with the individual who is changing. If this happens to you, it's more important than ever to stay focused on the prize, which is real, meaningful, and long-lasting empowerment and freedom. Hopefully, in time, those onlookers might start interacting with you in a more functional manner. If they see positive change, joy, and confidence in you, they just might want some for themselves and start unconsciously mirroring your behaviour!

In this process, you'll find that you start to become a different person – a more peaceful and connected version of yourself. You'll attract people who are supportive of you and in whom you bring out the best. You'll also gain the strength to move away from people who are no longer good for you.

You can embrace your family or cultural traditions that are healthy and supportive, but you don't have to let them define who you are and everything you do. Change can be difficult, but if you power through, you'll come out the other side stronger. You might find that you're now the person who attracts positive people and situations. Take courage from the fact that by having been brave, happy, and grateful, and having been on others' Dream Teams, you've already started to have an impact on those around you.

Last, don't worry; you don't have to tell anyone about your dreams yet, although you're nearly there. Dreaming big is still the creative time before you make concrete plans, and this is the quiet side of empowerment.

Dreamy Umbrellas

Imagine your life as an umbrella where the canopy represents your dreams. The struts, spokes, and supports are formed by all the permissions you've given yourself, the experiences you have gained, and the goals and actions you've aimed for. When the structure of the umbrella is in place, you can release the mechanism, and your dreams will take shape as the umbrella opens. We generally buy an umbrella because it appeals to us aesthetically; we like it for some reason. My favourite one is black on the outside but has a multi-coloured lining. Everyone else sees the black shell, but I see a rainbow when I look up! So when we buy that fun umbrella, we don't even give a thought to the complex mechanism that holds it up, but without its structure, the canopy would just be a tangle of material. It may still be attractive, but it's ultimately useless as an umbrella.

I think it's motivating to design the fabric first so you can visualise your secure shelter and get excited by the process of reaching your goal of creating the perfect umbrella. You already have the handle and shaft in place having travelled the Permission Journey (see chapter three). The struts, spokes, and supports, which consist of actions and goals, can be added after you fashion your dreams into the material of the canopy.

So, it's now time to imprint the fabric of your umbrella with images of your dream.

Moving from Dreaming to Doing

Definiteness of purpose is the starting
point of all achievement.
—W. Clement Stone

Dreams are very important, but only insofar as they give us the inspiration and focus we need to envision and work towards goals. They help you give yourself permission to live the life you want and to do the things that make you happy and fulfilled by showing you what the future could look like. But, if we go back and look at Louise Hay's quote "Awareness is fifty percent of growth", we have to look at what the other fifty percent looks like. It is all well and good being self-aware, but to really grow into the life and person you want to be, you have to take action – and that is the other fifty percent.

This is the stage when you start translating your dreams into realisable goals. It's easier to move into action when we have specific aims to work towards. They don't have to be huge dream-like goals, though; they can be little goals at first. If your goal is to improve your writing skills, that's not going to happen overnight, but you can start by aiming to read five of the great classics so that you can gain familiarity with well-written work. If your dream were to climb a mountain, what goals would you have to put in place to realise that? If you currently get out of breath climbing the stairs in your office building, your very first goal could be to climb all the stairs without getting puffed.

Now is the time for you to start exploring the many good books and programs out there on goal setting and action planning. Attend lectures, join groups, participate in webinars and online training programs, listen to podcasts, or do whatever works for you to crystallise your goals and work towards them. It's often helpful to be accountable to others, such as a community group, a coach, a colleague, or a friend. Revisit your Dream Team and identify which members you're accountable to. Ensure that you continue to give yourself permission to engage in the thoughts, behaviours, and dreams that are authentic to what you want for your life.

A Shortcut: The Permission Trifecta

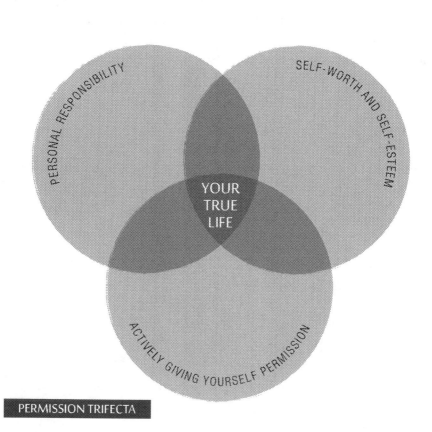

PERMISSION TRIFECTA

Figure 12:1: The Permission Trifecta

We are able to dream big most successfully from our authentic selves. I believe we can only access our real gut instincts when we come from a place of truly believing in and caring for ourselves. However, at first, we might have to employ a few shortcuts!

The *World English Dictionary* describes a trifecta as "any achievement involving three successful outcomes." With this in mind, I propose that you become successful in the following outcomes:

- actively give yourself permission
- take personal responsibility for your life
- believe that you matter (experience self-worth and self-esteem)

When all three of the above happen (Figure 12:1), you're very much on the way to living the life you want and deserve. Each of these outcomes relies on the others. If you're successful in all three, you have an increased chance of achieving your desired life. Each concept can be attained independently from the others, but each is also bolstered by the mastery of the other two.

Sometimes you have to trick yourself into giving yourself permission to do something, whether you believe you're worthy or not. See figure 12:2 below for a way to do this. In so doing, you take personal responsibility, and when you've done that, you then give yourself permission to do supportive things for yourself. All of this becomes a lot easier if you believe you're worth it.

The three concepts illustrated in Figure 12:1 take part in a very delicate, finely balanced dance. Sometimes one is a stronger partner than the other, sometimes each performs a solo, but the show is really at its best when all three are on stage, dancing with each other in harmonious synchronicity.

Exercise: Permission Slip

I see *actively* giving yourself permission as akin to forcing yourself to do something. Here is one way of achieving this.

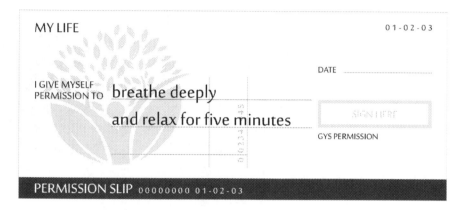

MY LIFE   01-02-03

DATE

I GIVE MYSELF
PERMISSION TO breathe deeply

and relax for five minutes   SIGN HERE

GYS PERMISSION

PERMISSION SLIP 00000000 01-02-03

Figure 12:2: Permission Slip

Write a permission slip if you're having difficulty with this concept. Either mock up a template on your computer or draw and handwrite one. Make it look like a certificate. If you make one on your computer, leave a blank space to write in what you want to give yourself permission for. You can also download a blank version of this permission slip from *www.GYSPermission. com.* You can print out a stack of blank permission slips and have them on hand and ready to use. I know this might sound a bit childish at first, but this is just a trick to get you started exercising the permission-giving muscle.

Staying True to Yourself

———ᴡᴏᴏᴄᴇᴛᴏᴏᴛᴇᴏᴏᴡ———

Don't ask yourself what the world needs; ask yourself what
makes you come alive. And then go and do that. Because
what the world needs is people who have come alive.
—Howard Thurman

———ᴡᴏᴏᴄᴇᴛᴏᴏᴛᴇᴏᴏᴡ———

When you've identified your goals, make sure they're consistent with
your dreams by ensuring that they're true to your most fundamental
values. One of my goals has been not to let MS stop me from doing
anything. Things might have to be modified, but I don't plan on ever
giving up entirely. Whenever I go for a medical check-up, which I need
to do periodically, I make a point of wearing really snazzy high heels.
The last thing I want is to feel like is a stereotype of the MS patient who
has problems with balance and fears falling over. The shoes represent
my values of independence and luxury. Whilst I sometimes have a few
balance issues and have been known to sprain both ankles in a single
day, I hope I never to have to wear those beige, flat, lace-up shoes
that people associate with the elderly or infirm. There are times when
I change back into stylish flat shoes outside the doctor's waiting room,
but at least I had my power shoes on at some point. This might sound
trivial, but for me it's all about taking responsibility for my mood and
how I feel about myself and about meeting my goals for freedom,
strength, and living in a way that is consistent with my values. I may
look cute, but I'm also making an effort and not giving in to the disease
and symptoms that are expected of an MS patient. There may be a point
in the future when I have to relinquish my heels and will need to find
another way to express these values and attain my goal of not allowing
MS to change who I fundamentally am. The truth is that I've had my
eye on a really stylish ebony and silver cane, but I don't need it yet.

It makes me happy when I see an elderly lady in a bright, carefully chosen outfit. I see her as the vibrant and wise person she is rather than the stereotypical old, frail individual who gives the impression of having lost sight of all her hopes and aspirations.

Always stay true to yourself and your values when you work towards your goals and dreams. Keep checking in with yourself; are you on the right path? When it feels right and you're happy, then go for what you want.

Holding On to Your Intention

—⁓⦿⦿⦿⦿⁓—

Life takes on meaning when you become motivated, set goals and charge after them in an unstoppable manner.
—Les Brown

—⁓⦿⦿⦿⦿⁓—

Holding on to your intention throughout both setting goals and taking action is very important. It's good to know what you want on a macro dream level, but it's often easier and more manageable to work towards incremental goals. At first I encourage clients to tackle the micro level and practise holding intention for smaller things.

For instance, be clear about what your intention is when you have a desired outcome for a particular conversation. If you're clear on that, you'll be better able to gauge any and all available opportunities to achieve it. They'll make themselves known to you. Having intention is all about knowing what you want and focusing on it, and then allowing whatever it is come to you. You just have to show up and position yourself in the most advantageous situation.

Seamus: A Story of Intention

A client of mine, Seamus, came to see me because he wanted to work on where his career was headed.

"I want my employer to give me more money," he explained.

Together, we explored whether more money was really what Seamus wanted, and he realised that what he was actually so anxious about was his desire for the people he worked with to see and appreciate how valuable he was to the organisation. The money represented this value.

When Seamus felt ready to have a conversation with his employers, he was confident that not only was he very valuable to the organisation but also that he was worth a lot more than he was being paid. He went into the meeting with this intention firmly in mind. As he was so clear and so full of conviction, he was in a position to confidently present the salary he desired. By holding this intention and because he truthfully *was* as valuable as he thought, he got the pay raise he wanted.

This may not always happen, but it can if you *sweep your side of the street* and position yourself in a place where you cannot be denied. Seamus had worked hard over the years and had put himself in a place where he deserved what he was asking for, so all he had to do was be specific about what he wanted and gain the courage to ask for it.

Jedi Mind Tricks

Star Wars is probably one of my favourite films, and when working on intention, I often suggest that my clients use Jedi mind tricks. This is in reference to the scene in the film when the Stormtroopers are looking for two specific droids and Obi-Wan Kenobi, a Jedi knight, is able to deflect them simply by saying with great conviction and influence, "These are not the droids you are looking for." Through his sureness alone, he's able to convince the Stormtroopers that it's true, that those are not the droids they were looking for, when, in fact, they were.

When you're going into a situation that you're unsure of or nervous about, you can apply a Jedi mind trick and draw confidence from your intention. I've learned that when I focus on positive outcomes and hold the intention for them, good things happen much more often. It's not all about focusing on what I want in the material world but on what I want to happen as an experience or occurrence.

Carlos: A Story of the Jedi Mind Trick in Action

One of my clients, Carlos, was about to buy a house but felt that the seller needed to lower the price by fifty thousand pounds (eighty thousand US dollars) to reflect remedial works that needed to be carried out (yes, London property prices are very high!). He was anxious about the meeting that had been arranged, and we discussed it in preparation. I asked him what his intention for the meeting was.

"Well, to get a lower price," he said.

"Why does the house warrant a lower price?" I asked.

He explained about all the work the house needed and how he felt that justified an appropriate price reduction.

"Okay," I said. "You know what you want and why. Exactly what is the intention for this meeting?"

"To get the seller to approve a fifty-thousand-pound reduction in the cost of the property because I'm going to have to spend that on things that should have already been done."

"Are you comfortable that that figure is appropriate?"

"Yes," he said.

"Right, then," I told him. "So you know what you want to do with this conversation. Keep that intention at the forefront of your mind. Your intention is 'I want this person to take off fifty thousand pounds'. Go and look the seller in the eye and think, 'I want to pay fifty thousand pounds less', and actually hold the full price you want to pay in your mind."

Carlos got the discount, bought the house, did a year's worth of renovations, and moved in.

When Things Change

—·····—

Progress is impossible without change, and those who
cannot change their minds cannot change anything.
—George Bernard Shaw

—·····—

As you work towards your goals, situations may change. The important thing here is to keep your intention without becoming inflexible. Possibly the route to your goal will be slightly different than you imagined, and that is okay.

Imagine it as shopping for a car. Sometimes you know exactly what you want – the make, the colour, the horsepower – and you have the money to go out and get it. But in general, you have to do some research, look around, compare online, ask for input from friends, read reviews, and test-drive various models beforehand. You may have thought you knew which car you wanted, but other factors start to affect your decision. The headrest in one car may have been unbearably uncomfortable, changing your decision entirely. Your goal was to buy a car, and your action was to do all the research and look for qualities that fit your personal needs. You now need to give yourself permission to change your mind if you come across a useful, new, game-changing piece of information. However, still keep the intention and goal of owning the best car for you in mind.

It's like that chess game – life runs well with some strategy. If you're purposeful in how you move your pieces and you have them in the right place at the right time in relation to others, you will win the game. You have ultimate control and responsibility over how you react or respond. You will get the life you want, but you have to have a strategy first, and you have to be willing to adjust it if the circumstances change.

Just like when you're in a positive state of mind and you visualise your desires concretely, you'll be more open to seeing the opportunities available to you. Bear in mind that intention is an internal, private way of articulating goals. Goals tend to be more external, whereas intentions are held in the recesses of your heart and mind.

Give YourSelf Permission to Live Your Life

You are now at a point where you give yourself permission to have dreams. You know that there will be challenges and that you'll always need to focus wholeheartedly on your intentions. It takes time to change the fundamental way you think. Many people have put themselves last for so many years that the changes they need to make can seem very foreign and, frankly, quite selfish. So, sometimes you have to fake it 'till you make it and force yourself to do something out of the ordinary because it might feel good in the long run. If nothing else, you've started laying the foundation for future growth and well-being.

The Permission Journey: Homeward Stage

Welcome back! As you travelled towards home in this stage, you have been able to dream big and have understood the power of intention. The journey itself is the process – everything you have become aware of, everything you have learned, and everything you have started to implement in your everyday life.

This place may look a little different from when you left, as you'll see it through new eyes. Your sense of worth and responsibility will lead to your ability to focus on the positive and change what you no longer choose to tolerate. Decisions and relationships will come easier once you start living by your values.

Here are a set of questions that allow you to gauge where you are and what you've learned.

These questions are slightly different from the previous ones, as they apply to your whole journey. They're here to elicit major celebration, and with your newfound dreams and power to live *your* life, you're now able to go forth and conquer.

1) What did you learn for and about yourself as you traveled the entire Permission Journey?
2) What tools or realisations are you going to live by from here on out?
3) What traits, behaviours, thoughts, or memories are you going to leave behind?

So now it's time to go back to the list you made in "Chapter Three: The Permission Journey" to see if what you wanted to give yourself permission to do is still valid. Is there anything you want to change? Is there anything you want to take away or add? Most importantly, though, is there anything you've already achieved or are ready to incorporate into your life right now? Now is the time; we have only a finite amount of time on earth, and every moment counts.

Conclusion

Freedom Is Yours

———⁓⬗⬖⬗⬖⬗⬖⬗⬖⬗⬖⬗⬖———

Stars when you shine you know how I feel,
scent of the pine you know how I feel, yeah
freedom is mine, and I know how I feel
—"Feeling Good" by Nina Simone

———⁓⬗⬖⬗⬖⬗⬖⬗⬖⬗⬖⬗⬖———

When you truly, wholeheartedly give yourself permission to do what you think is right and be who you want to be, you are capable of infinite achievements. Not only will you enjoy yourself that much more, but you will also believe in what you are doing. This is freedom.

Freedom *looks* different for everyone. To some it might be travelling the world all on their own for many years or having a huge family of children and grandchildren to explore life with. However, freedom *feels* the same for most people. When living freely, you know that you have made hard choices but have also made the right decisions for yourself. You know that you may have made some mistakes but you also know that you can live with them because you did the best you knew how at the time. You should be quietly proud of yourself.

Freedom is taking personal responsibility. When you blame others for how you feel, you completely incarcerate yourself in the prison of others' actions. Only you hold the key that opens the gates that free you to make a dash for the wide-open world. Holding resentment and anger towards others is the least freeing thing you can do. But, once out in the open air, you can pick the path that will allow you to be free – free to carry on making healthy choices. In a way, it's a domino effect: once you put one productive action into place, it makes the next one easier to activate.

Freedom allows you to live in the present. Being present means that you appreciate every moment you live, at the time it happens. They might not all be good, but you can learn and grow from these situations. When you are present in where you are and what you are doing, you are much more open and available to recognising and taking advantage of supportive opportunities – opportunities that will perpetuate your experience of who you really are. You will be living y*our* life.

Also, being present in your life will help you see those around you for who they are and enable you to support them the way you see fit. You will see where they shine, and you can appreciate them for that. This genuine support and love for others will be apparent to those around you, and they will be drawn to you.

Sometimes you can't do everything alone and you have to ask for help. You cannot expect anyone to fix your problems, but by sharing a little of the burden, you can free yourself to catch your breath and look around for better ways to get out of the quagmires you sometimes find yourself in. Your Dream Team members support you, and that allows you much freedom, and you can do the same for them.

Even though the first step of the journey is to give yourself permission to know you matter, it is often very difficult to do when you don't feel free, and it's near impossible to be free if you don't think you matter. This is a vicious circle that needs to be broken at some point. So by travelling the first stage of the journey, you have proved to yourself that you do matter enough, and it's up to you to keep up the good work.

You also experience freedom both personally and professionally when you give yourself permission to live in accordance with your values. You will *know* that you are doing the right thing, and that will allow you to be much more at peace with your decisions and therefore be more present in your life, in the lives of others, and the communities you live and work in.

Laughing with friends and having fun in general can lighten the soul, even if just for a few moments. Those moments build on each other, and all of a sudden you realise that you have had a great deal of fun, and you go to sleep happy and carefree. It can't be this way *all* the time, but it can be this way *much* of the time if you just choose to grab hold of the peace and centredness joy provides.

You can live your whole life seeking freedom from fear because fear is one of the most crippling feelings. What would you do with your life if you weren't afraid to fail? Now is the time to give yourself permission to try it! Freedom is deciding to take as large or as small a step as you're comfortable with to reach the goals and live the dreams you aspire to. In time, you just might risk taking bigger and bolder steps.

You will only be able to truly recognise opportunities if you know what they look like. By dreaming big and holding intention for what you absolutely believe to be beneficial and empowering for yourself, your loved ones, your job, your business, your co-workers, or your employees, you will be able to live life to its fullest, and this can only free you.

Let's see if we can create a rich tapestry of experience, fulfilment, and joy that will brighten this world. Quietly (or maybe not so quietly), give yourself permission to do or be anything you feel to be right, and see what happens. What will you achieve when you simply give yourself permission? We would all love to see you live your authentic and best life, the one every human being deserves to live.

We are nothing without our joy to live and our freedom. We will always regret not taking a stand when we could have. Don't let this opportunity pass you by.

Now go *celebrate*! Live *your* life and join the Freedom Revolution!

Epilogue

Most people have heard the name Rosa Parks. In 1955, Mrs Parks was travelling home from work on a bus in Montgomery, Alabama, when a white bus driver told her to leave her seat and give it to a white passenger because all the seats in the white section of the bus were filled. Mrs Parks, whose dream was already of an America in which all citizens were treated equally, regardless of colour, refused. And in that moment, the civil rights movement started to coalesce around her.

At the time of her arrest, Rosa Parks was working as a seamstress and holding down a voluntary position as the secretary of the local chapter of the National Association for the Advancement of Coloured People (NAACP). She had trained in the field of workers' rights and racial equality. Her dream must have been pretty clearly defined. On the bus, by holding the intention of the relatively small goal of not giving up her seat to someone just because he was white and she was not, she ignited a flame that is still burning to this day.

Many years later when she was sharing the events of that day she said, "When that white driver stepped back toward us, when he waved his hand and ordered us up and out of our seats, I felt a determination cover my body like a quilt on a winter night."[16]

Mrs Parks went on to receive the NAACP's Spingarn Medal in 1979, the Presidential Medal of Freedom, and the Congressional Gold Medal. In the 1980s, by the time she was approaching retirement age, Mrs Parks was involved in setting up a scholarship fund for university students and bus tours that taught a new generation about the civil rights movement. Her memoir, *Quiet Strength*, was published in 1995.

Mrs Parks passed away in 2005. She was the first woman to lie in honour in the US Capitol Rotunda. Flags were flown at half-mast in America on the day of her funeral. Today, a statue of her sits in the US Capitol's National Statuary Hall.

Whilst we might not all play a pivotal role in human and civil rights as Rosa Parks did, we *can* all follow her example. As an intelligent, engaged woman living in America in a time of crippling social division, her *dream* was of a nation in which all citizens were treated equally. Rosa Parks did not assume her personal goal to be the transformation of her whole society, but she was able to take small and meaningful steps towards this and to take personal responsibility for her own actions. In her case, one brave gesture, her realised goal not to relinquish her bus seat, did not go unnoticed; it was the catalyst for a movement that changed the face of American society. It started in 1955, when one small woman gave herself permission to say *no*.

---

[16]   http://www.biographyonline.net/humanitarian/rosa-parks.html

Further Reading

Life loves to be taken by the lapel and
told, "I'm with you kid. Let's go!"
—Maya Angelou

Books

Achor, Shawn. *The Happiness Advantage: the Seven Principles of Positive Psychology that Fuel Success and Performance at Work.* Virgin Books. 2011.

Byrne, Rhonda. *The Secret.* Simon and Schuster Ltd. 2006.

de Becker, Gavin. *The Gift of Fear: Survival Signals that Protect Us from Violence,* new edition, Bloomsbury Publishing PLC. 2000.

Deida, David. *The Way of the Superior Man.* Sounds True, Inc. 2004.

De Martini, John. *The Breakthrough Experience: A Revolutionary New Approach to Personal Transformation.* Hay House. 2002.

De Martini, John. *From Stress to Success in 31 Days.* Hay House. 2009.

Hay, Louise L. *You Can Heal Your Life,* 2nd ed. 2011.

Hay, Louise L. *Heal Your Body.* Hay House. 2004.

Holden, Robert. *Success Intelligence: Essential Lessons and Practices from the World's Leading Coaching Programme on Authentic Success.* Hay House. 2009

Northrop, Christiane. *Women's Bodies, Women's Wisdom.* Piatkus. 2009.

Tolle, Eckhart. *A New Earth: Awakening to Your Life's Purpose.* Penguin. 2008.

Websites

http://www.hayhouse.com – A website dedicated to the publishing house founded by Louise L. Hay.

http://www.hayhouseradio.com – The Hay House internet radio site.

http://www.cherylrichardson.com – The website of *New York Times* best-selling author Cheryl Richardson.

http://www.drwaynedyer.com – The website of self-help author and coach Wayne Dyer.

https://drdemartini.com – The website of Dr John De Martini, American researcher and coach.

http://www.hoffman-international.com – The Hoffman Process is an intensive 8-day residential course that promotes personal discovery and development.

http://www.mssociety.org.uk – the UK Multiple Sclerosis Society.

http://www.nationalmssociety.org – the US Multiple Sclerosis Society.

http://www.aa.org – The international Alcoholics Anonymous website.

http://www.al-anon.org – The Al-Anon Website (for friends and family of problem drinkers)

Acknowledgements

Thank you to all my friends and family for putting up with me and my incessant talk about 'the book', and for offering another set of eyes when I needed it! Thank you Deirdre and Kate for getting me started and thank you to all my wonderful interns from USC who edited and proofed up a storm.

Special heads-up to Jamie for reading the manuscript more times than anyone else and my mother, Cecelia, for being the fastest reader and my biggest cheerleader.

If I were to say *thank you* to everyone by name who has supported and helped me during this process, the list would be longer than the book itself! I am truly humbled and grateful.

Give YourSelf
Permission™

Through her work, Priya offers a guiding hand as you make your way through the Permission Journey™ – remember that you are not travelling alone. If you wish to delve deeper into each stage, or need added support, visit *www.GYSPermission.com*. Here you will find supplementary materials, e-courses, video and audio downloads, and more. More information and material will be added all the time, so come back and visit often. You will also find information on group workshops, public speaking, and private sessions.

Happy Travels!

WWW.GYSPERMISSION.COM

About the Author

P riya Rana Kapoor is a life coach and the founder of Give YourSelf Permission™, a program designed to foster foundational and long lasting self-awareness and empowerment.

Priya grew up in London, England and then spent over a decade in California mostly earning an undergraduate degree in theatre and a master's in marriage and family therapy, both from the University of Southern California (USC). Her post-grad research was in Alzheimer's and Parkinson's disease along with providing therapy to patients and their families at USC University Hospital's Department of Neurology and Neurosurgery. She is also a graduate of the Coach U Core Essentials Program.

Priya speaks to corporate and non-profit groups, facilitates workshops, and has appeared on NBC's Today Show where she was invited to discuss women's health issues.

As a vocal advocate for MS research, Priya is dedicated to helping the community through her work with the National MS Society. Additionally, her philanthropic commitment includes involvement with Aids Project

Los Angeles and the Junior League of Los Angeles and London. She also serves on the board of the USC Alumni Club of London.

Priya currently lives in London, but commutes to Los Angeles to speak, work with clients and visit with family and friends. She hopes to travel more, visit new countries and learn as much as she can from different cultures.